My American Dream

Autobiography of Won Ho Chang

Won Ho Chang, Ph.D.

Emeritus Professor of Journalism

University of Missouri

9 781312 333413

South Korea

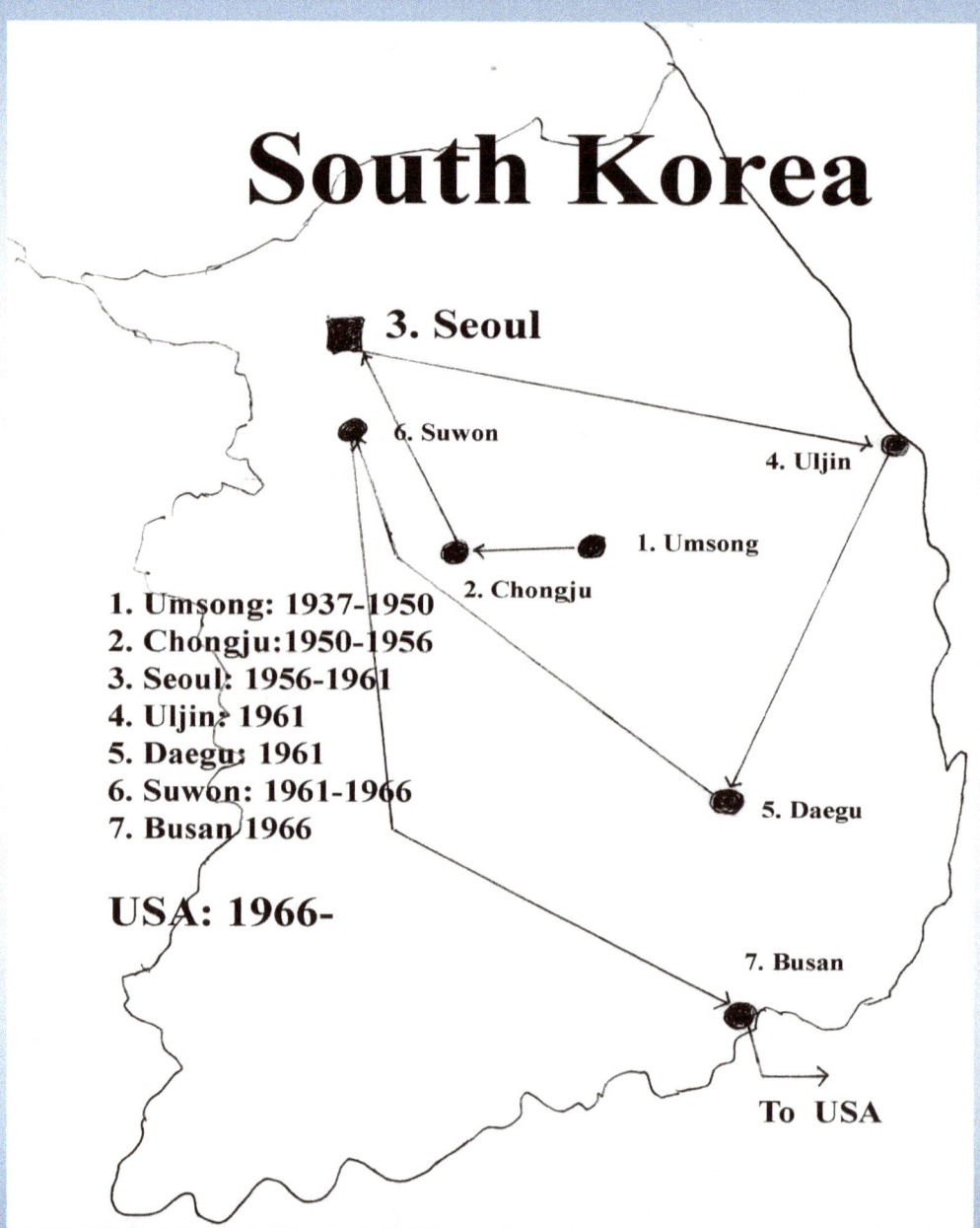

3. Seoul

6. Suwon

4. Uljin

1. Umsong

2. Chongju

1. Umsong: 1937-1950
2. Chongju:1950-1956
3. Seoul: 1956-1961
4. Uljin: 1961
5. Daegu: 1961
6. Suwon: 1961-1966
7. Busan 1966

USA: 1966-

5. Daegu

7. Busan

To USA

Contents

Preface

I was born in a rural town, Umsong, South Korea in 1937, was educated and had a successful career as a distinguished professor of journalism at the University of Missouri USA. Throughout and especially in these years of retirement, I have traveled all over the world.

I was heavily motivated to be a scholar at a very young age by my grandfather who had a vision based in the Confucian values and philosophy, which emphasized personal and governmental morality, correctness of social relationships, justice and sincerity.

I was told by my grandfather that my life's destiny came under the sign of the "running horse," which would carry me around the world. The source of this Confucian prophecy, The Book of Changes, considers the cycle of one life span to be 60 years. I have now surpassed that cycle by over two decades, but my destiny continues to keep me running. This book is an examination of that destiny and looks back at what I have done to accomplish my goals of AMERICAN DREAM along the way.

My first goal was to achieve the highest level of education. I began that journey in provincial high school in Chongju, Korea, eventually making my way to Seoul, Korea for college. After four years of preparation after graduating from Korea University, I made my way to Eugene, Oregon to take another bachelor's degree in journalism.

Then I moved down to Los Angeles for my master's and finally to Iowa City for my ultimate goal, a doctoral degree. It took me 35 years of hard work to achieve that goal.

My second goal was to be successful in my career. My career was centered on the teaching of journalism at the University of Missouri. I was honored to be awarded the O.O McIntire Distinguished Chair Professorship and worked as a department chair, director of the Stephenson Research Center and associate dean for graduate studies and research. I supervised 33 doctoral dissertations, wrote 16 books, spearheaded the use of word processing in printing newspapers, helped to establish and modernize newspapers in Asia and mentored a young journalists all over the world.

My third goal was to have a successful family life. My wife Young and I have been happily married for 61 years. We have been blessed to have three children who are well educated, happily married and successful in their careers: Susan works as a City Planner, and her husband, David, has an architectural firm. They live with their sons Ben and Eric in British Columbia, Canada; Anthony, a senior international attorney for a law firm, lives with his wife, Damee, in Seoul, Korea with their children, Alex and Chloe; and Eugene is a professor at Emerson College in Boston, and his wife, Tessa also is a professor and department chair at Wheaton College in Norton Massachusetts. They live in the Boston area with their son, Tobin.

Now, as a retiree, I have settled in a retirement community, Laguna Woods Village in California. My destiny, however is keeping me running. I work as a leader of a traveling group of retirees and am traveling around the world searching for renewed meaning to my life in retirement. I also have been reading many books, both fiction and non-fiction, which I could not do when I was immersed in my academic research and teaching. I am also enjoying the natural wonders of the surrounding mountains and beaches and practicing my favorite sports, golf and fishing. What meaning does my life hold for me now? I am running to explore this question in the pages that follow.

Laguna Woods Village

August, 2023

Part 1. The Beginning

From 1947 Class Picture

1. Home Town
(Umsong)

I was born on April 27, 1937, in Umsong South Korea as the first child of the 34th generation of the In-dong clan of the CHANG family. Our ancestor started this family around the year 1070 during the Koryo Kingdom.

My great-great grandfather was a military general who retired to a small village called Kwansung, about 10 miles north of Umsong. My great grandfather joined the "Uprising of the Eastern Learning Peasant Army" in 1894.

The Eastern Learning combined aspects of Buddhist meditation, Confucian ethics, Shamanistic knowledge of nature and Taoist cultivation of energy. He returned to his hometown, but many of his followers were killed during the fight with government soldiers and their families demanded compensation from their leader.

The Eastern Learning was not only a religious movement but a social movement as well and was concerned with the peasantry and the improvement of their conditions and reforming the corrupt government. The idea of the dignity and equality of all men was to influence future democratic movements. The initial success of the revolt led a panicked court to seek help from China and Japan, leading to the first Sino-Japanese War and eventually to Japanese colonization of Korea.

At the age of 30, our great grandfather lost most of his estate and property and died, leaving a young son. At a young age, my grandfather kept about 10 acres on the mountain slopes where our ancestors were buried, and moved to Umsong, where he started working for a small rice store and later became the owner and operator of a rice and barley mill.

The home town of my grandfather, Kwan-sung village, was the setting of a sad story about a couple of storks that nested on a big tree planted by my great grandfather on the side of a small lake. During the sixties, an illegal hunter shot and killed the male bird, leaving behind the widowed hen.

The poor bird could not find her mate and was so disconsolate that her eggs were never hatched. Mass media in Korea followed this sad story, and many Koreans around the country felt the pain and sadness of this lovely but sad big bird. About five years later, the hen died, and no other stork came to the town again, leaving this now legendary story lodged in the minds of the people in a small rural town in Korea.

Kwan-sung is now a suburb of Umsong, where I was born and my grandfather succeeded in becoming a relatively wealthy factory and land owner. Thanks must go to my grandfather who saved the mountain acreage in Kwan-sung where many of my ancestors, including my grandparents and parents are buried. Our family can visit the town and pay our respects to our ancestors for laying an inspirational foundation for us.

As a successful businessman, my grandfather established his estate and reputation. He and his wife had two children, my father and a younger daughter. My aunt married a businessman in a nearby town but died at the age of 30 without leaving any children. My father was born in 1914. He was educated and trained by his father and was forced to marry a stranger who was one year older than himself when he was just 15. My grandfather explained to us that it was his intention to have as many grandchildren as possible by having his only son marry at that tender age.

After the wedding ceremony, my father rebelled against his father by leaving the town abruptly, without his new young bride. He headed to Manchuria, China, where he stayed for the next five years. As the Japanese colonial government in Korea tightened its grip and expanded its invasion into Manchuria, my father came back to Umsong in 1934 and started working for his father. My mother had stayed with the Chang family during her husband's five-year absence, and was reunited with a grown-up husband.

After eight years of marriage, my father had his first son, me, in 1937. Even though things did not work out as my grandfather expected, my grandparents were extremely delighted by the arrival of a new family member, who would head the 34th generation of the Chang family. During the time when my mother was pregnant, my grandparents had provided my mother with a number of expensive herbal medicines such as ginseng and elk's horn.

My mother repeatedly explained to me later that I was allergic to the herbal medicine. The newborn baby was big, but he had a high fever and a terrible skin rash all over his body. Anxious about the health problem, my grandfather visited many famous physicians for help, but the baby's condition only worsened, and he was told that the baby was not going to survive.

It took more than three months for me to show signs of improvement, and only then did my father decide to register my birthday in the county office. I was born on April 27, but my registered birthday is August 10, which has remained my official birthday. However, I have been very healthy after those early problems, and my mother used to tell me that I eventually benefited a great deal from the herbal medicine she took while she was pregnant.

I was taken care of extremely well by my grandparents. I was moved to a separate residential area of my grandparents when my first younger brother was born in December 1940 and stayed with them for 10 years until I was sent to a middle school in Chongju, the capital of Chungbuk Province, about 26 miles from my hometown.

My grandparents were delighted to have eight grandchildren, five boys and three girls. It was an old tradition that the first grandson, designated to be the successor of the head of the family, was cared for by his grandparents who

When I was only four years old, I was taught Chinese characters and literature by my grandfather who was well respected by the town's people. With long white hair and a beard, my grandfather was often invited to settle family disputes. I benefited most from his vision and teaching of the Confucian values and traditions. When I was only six, I could write ancestor memorial service material in Chinese. This training was very unusual among Korean people of my time.

Decades later, I visited a former grade school classmate whose father had died the night before. In a small rural town, nobody seemed to know how to write traditional funeral eulogies in Chinese. When I volunteered to do that, everybody there was shocked by the fact that an American professor who had been living in the States for more than 20 years still remembered the Chinese texts.

My grandfather also taught me how to write names according to the system developed to identify the generation of each person. The basic principle of this system follows the sequence and cycle of the five elements of the universe:

metal produces water which produces wood which produces fire which produces earth which produces metal again. Each person's name contains one of these five components in the first or second character. Based on this system, ten generations can be easily identified, and there should be no confusion in the names of a respectable family. I was taught to write names of our family as well as any other Korean family, and I could identify the heritages of many well-established families in Korea.

In 1944, as the Second World War was being fought in the Pacific area, I had to take a simple entrance examination to enter the first grade of the Japanese-style grade school. We were forced to use only the Japanese language until the Japanese surrendered on August 15, 1945. We did not know then how desperate the military leaders of the Japanese empire were as they began to realize they could not win the war as they had planned and would soon pay the price.

Japan had begun a desperate final campaign to win the war when I started grade school and my classmates and I were swept up in the fervor of this ultimately futile last attempt. We were forced to visit the Japanese shrine early every morning before school and scream our oaths to the Japanese emperor. An active-duty Japanese sergeant in full military uniform with sword drilled us in the military fashion, and forced us to perform our "patriotic" duties. This consisted of collecting all the metal kitchen utensils and other metal ware to make ammunition, cultivating our gardens and any available lands for food, and doing military exercises almost every day.

As the end of the war approached in the first months of 1945, civil defense exercises were added to the daily routine, and we dug hideout bunkers in the house as well as in public places, including the schools. American B-29 bombers were seen in our town but they never dropped any bomb on Korean soil. As a second grader, I was confused about what was going on. My grandfather said Japan was about to lose the war, but the Japanese teachers were insisting to the end on imminent victory.

On the fifteenth of August, Japan surrendered, and most of the Japanese people on the Korean peninsula were shipped back to the Japanese islands. However, the end of Japanese colonial rule brought great turmoil to Korea. I witnessed many pivotal historical events through my eight-year-old eyes. The sudden departure of all Japanese officials left the enormous task of maintaining law and order to the local people who claimed that they fought against Japanese colonial rule.

Seoul in 1945

After the end of Japanese rule, the American military occupied the nation south of the 38th parallel while the North was occupied by Soviet troops, marking the beginning of the tragic division of the Korean peninsula. During my school days, as a second grader, I watched many Japanese-made war movies, where American soldiers were depicted as cowards and fools with big shoes and noses. When we actually met American soldiers, liberators of the Korean people from Japanese rule, we discovered a completely different image of Americans, who brought medicine, some school supplies and lots of American candies.

There were, of course, many political parties in Korea, including the Communist Party built by the people who actively participated in the independence movement and who joined the international communist movement in 1922. The party thought of itself as the leader of the independent country of Korea, but it suddenly became the enemy of the American supporters and their followers.

I was terribly confused about this complicated ideological struggle. Their fights sometimes were so fierce that some of the Communist members were beaten to death in front of onlookers. The roots of anti-Americanism started about this time. Dependents and children of Communists were killed or persecuted. Very few Communists were appointed to be high-ranking government or military officials.

Troubled by the fierce ideological struggles, American military forces in the southern half of the Korean peninsula sided with Syngman Rhee for the establishment of the first Republic of Korea in 1948 and supported him to bring law and order to the country. Rhee was indeed our national patriotic leader whom Korea was privileged to have. Rhee was born in 1875 and died at the age of 91 in Hawaii. The fact is that the first president of the Republic is not recognized like George Washington in the United States, because most of the monuments in his honor were destroyed by radical political groups.

Rhee was sent to America at the age of 29 to complete his education from distinguished universities: He received a B.A. from George Washington University, his M.A. from Harvard and his Ph.D. in political science from Princeton. He worked for the independence of his homeland and deserved to be the first president of the country.

President Rhee did not have many options but to rehire former policemen and collaborationist government workers under Japanese rule in order to establish a functioning government. The first principles of his rule were anti-Communist and anti-Japanese.

Our mill was expanded to establish a second factory and our family was doing exceptionally well. We processed rice and barley, produced wheat flour, and deseeded cotton to process it for weaving textiles. We even extracted oil from the cottonseed, and manufactured rough soaps for washing clothes.

As a boy from an affluent family, I was admired by many. One sunny afternoon in May 1947, we fourth graders were gathered under a huge tree outside our classroom and our teacher Choi unexpectedly asked us what we would like to do in life. I told the class that I would become a diplomat, a career young small town boys were not even allowed to dream about. I was able to entertain such notions because my grandfather had inspired me ever since I was just four years old.

Kyungsoo, a close friend of mine, surprised us all by saying that he would become a municipal administrator, a job his father held at that time. Kyungsoo, nicknamed henceforth the "Municipal Administrator," was an over-protected only child who was never permitted to swim in deep waters or to climb high mountains. He

drowned in a lake when he was trying to learn how to swim on his own. He was only a junior in high school.

I appreciated my grandfather's teachings. He actively taught me how to swim and how to skate, among other things. He explained that there would be many tough situations in my future and that I should learn to overcome such difficulties through physical strength, perseverance and humility. Throughout my adventures in the States, I often thought about my grandfather's words whenever I was faced with tough and difficult challenges.

The rural town of Umsong, where the county government was located, had a population of about 10,000 in 1920s. Two rugged mountains, Kayup and Sungjae, fenced the northern and eastern sides of town. But the town became a booming industrial center in 1920, when the Japanese authorities who became interested in tobacco in Umsong County developed it with two other surrounding counties, Chungju, and Jinchon. On account of this tobacco cultivation, the town was modernized much earlier than most other towns by the Japanese in their exploitation of Korean resources. The booming town was a collecting place for green tobacco, and a government agency dried, and then transported it back to Japan or to other cigarette plants.

For this reason, the Umsong railroad station was built on the western side of town, from where a steam-engine locomotive train whistled early in the morning, awaking the entire town. From 1920 to 1945, tobacco was one of the major agricultural products the Japanese intended to grow on the colonial Korean peninsula. Japan found the Umsong area best suited for tobacco growing and urged Korean farmers to participate in "new farming" with many financial incentives.

Tobacco growing was a labor-intensive activity, and there was plenty of labor from many Korean farming towns. The Umsong area was known as the best place to grow so-called "Yellow Tobacco." Sometime in the autumn tobacco leaves were collected and dried in a wood burning drier before being sent to about 20 huge warehouses located right next to the railroad station.

Farmers brought tobacco to the Japanese authorities and traded it for a relatively large amount of cash that many rural townspeople had never seen before. The large amount of cash brought to this farming town had both good and bad consequences. Many people had opportunities to see what modern industry could bring into town and how modernized people lived, sending their children to school and traveling to the larger cities in Japan.

Growing up as a young child, I also was a beneficiary of this development. My parents repeatedly told me that I should go to Japan. I was highly motivated to move on from a small rural town to bigger cities for education and for a career. The Japanese tobacco industry, however, also brought the unsavory side of capital to the town. Umsong was invaded by gamblers, brokers and prostitutes, and the locals lost not only a large amount of cash to tobacco and its byproducts but also their farmlands. My grandparents, with whom I had lived through my grade school years, were visited by their friends, who exchanged their stories of gambling and prostitution. My grandfather had been shocked by my interest in listening to such "bad stories," but he could not keep my ears shielded from such stories.

The Japanese school year started the first week of April, and I was seven years old when I was admitted to a public grade school after passing the entrance examination, which consisted of an IQ test and physical examination. Students were forced to speak Japanese, but continued to speak Korean at home.

There were separate classes for the first grade for boys and girls. Following the guidelines of the educational system in Japan, boys and girls were strictly segregated while playing or engaging in school activities.

But after the liberation from Japan in 1945, I was assigned to an integrated classroom, where boys were separated from girls by a walkway.

In fourth grade, I found myself attracted to a girl by the name of Nam and sometimes exchanged a few words with her about homework. Nam's family ran an apple orchard and her father was a good friend of my father's, but we never visited each other's homes.

Each year there were a few class picnics, during which the whole class packed lunches and water (no other drinks were available to us) and walked four miles to a scenic area, ate our lunches, played a few games, and then walked back to school.

During the 1948 spring picnic, Nam brought me a few apples and some hard-boiled eggs, which was a special treat at that time, and tried to put them into my lunch bag when I was wasn't looking. Some jealous boys noticed our friendship and began to spread the news as if ours was the biggest romantic affair in the school. Nam and I were so traumatized by the harassment that we never again came close to each other after that. In fact, for years after that I didn't talk to girls unless it was absolutely necessary.

Umsong

1956

2. High School
(Chongju)

I started my education at Su-bong Primary School, the only public school in Umsong which had been founded around 1910 by the Japanese authorities. During colonial rule, a limited number of schools were established and a selected group of children were accepted into them by entrance examination.

After 1945, however, all school-age children or older were required to go to school. Some of my classmates, therefore, were a few years older than I, and the size of my class in 1945 was about 70 instead of the normal size of 40. Even though I didn't learn the Korean alphabet until the second grade, I did exceptionally well in the class by scoring the highest in most examinations.

Chongju Middle School was the oldest and best school in our province, and only the top dozen students at Umsong School were allowed to apply for admission. According to the teachers, only two could pass the entrance examination in a good year, and none in a bad year. 1950 was an average year when I was the only one out of twelve applicants from the school who passed the examination.

The good news made my grandfather very happy. I can still remember how my grandfather showed his happiness. He immediately ordered a big pig for a party and invited all the school teachers and his friends for the celebration. This legendary episode about my grandfather is still one of the favorite stories among the folks of Umsong.

I was very popular among friends, since I was the only one from our town attending Chongju Middle School. And I enjoyed my grandfather's generosity which provided me with many luxury items such as leather school shoes instead of canvas.

The first semester of school started on April 1, as established by the Japanese. I went into a totally new environment where I knew none of my 300 classmates. Before settling in a boarding house in Chongju, I had to commute 26 miles from Umsong by train, which took about one and a half hours to travel. A coal burning steam-engine locomotive with four passenger coaches stopped at four stations before reaching my destination, Chongju. There were about a dozen older students from Umsong station, most of them were older than I, but we were joined by hundreds of students. While we normally could not find an empty seat, but it was a really exciting hour for a thirteen-year-old boy. After six hours, we were scheduled to take the train again at around five o'clock in the afternoon to come back home.

It had been only three months into the routine of commuting and schooling until the day North Korea invaded the South on June 25, 1950. Most of South Korea was occupied by North Korean troops except for a small corner of the peninsula in the Southeast. During the three-month occupation by the North Korean army, I was hiding with my grandparents in a small mountain town. I neither saw massive numbers of North Korean troops nor participated in North Korean youth activities.

I was very lucky to be only 13 and not a physically big boy to be drafted into the North Korean army. Many young students were forced to "volunteer" in the North Korean army and died in the conflict. The school was closed for more than three months until the first week of October when the South Korean army with the help of troops sent by the United Nations pushed the invaders all the way to the Yalu River and Manchuria. Then, the Chinese army with massive manpower joined the conflict and our troops retreated to where the current 38th parallel line is. Most of the bridges and rail tracks were bombed and destroyed, and I had to ride a bicycle to travel 26 miles. I later lived with my father's friend, whose house was located by the middle school.

My father was doing exceptionally well in 1950, obtaining permission from the military to transport rice and other grains to Seoul where no civilians were allowed to travel without permission from the Korean military. We owned four trucks, and my grandfather sometimes assigned one truck to go to Chongju to pick me up for a weekend stay with him.

As the only Umsong country boy in the school and due to the closing of school for three months, I did not have a close friend in the school until one October day when I met Manjo.

We were first graders at Chongju Middle School, and we quickly became the closest of friends and have continued to be ever since. He came from a small town in Bo-un County under the Sock-Ri Mountain. The house he was staying in belonged to his uncle who worked for the provincial court. Manjo had many relatives and cousins in Chongju. I became a close friend of his folks.

One afternoon in October of 1950, one of our trucks needed to be painted in Chongju, and I went to the paint shop to see the truck driver, whom I always called Uncle. Manjo lived in a house next to the paint shop. When we met for the first time, we could easily see that we were in the same grade in the same school. We used to wear uniforms, on which we had our name tags and grade signs just like in the military.

1954 on the West Gate Stone Bridge

Manjo and I were quickly introduced to two new friends: Keyjung and Kwangsook, and formed "the Gang of Four," as we were known by our classmates in those days.

The Kwangsook family was from Cheju Island and had four sons. The oldest brother was a Harvard graduate and was teaching political science at Connecticut State University in the fifties. The second brother was preparing for his study in the United States.

High School Friends in 1955

Manjo and I lived in a boarding house across a narrow street from Kwangsook's house and spent most of our time after school with Kwangsook and his second brother who tried to encourage us to study English. He even persuaded us to read English books that were far more difficult than our school textbooks. Manjo and I were doing exceptionally well with the English subjects, and I benefited a lot from this opportunity to learn English. I was motivated to go to the United States. When I mentioned my intention of going to America, my parents and friends just laughed at me. However, my grandfather was really excited about the idea since he was convinced about my future diplomatic career, as predicted by his friend.

Keyjung, one other friend from Seoul, decided to stay in Chongju even after he was allowed to move back to his original school because his elder brother was a chief of police in Chungju County. In secondary school, Keyjung, a tall, handsome and rich city boy, who had many female admirers. We all got heavily involved in social activities instead of working hard on school work.

I was shocked by the news of the death of my greatest sponsor, my grandfather. I was a junior in high school, and I felt like I lost everything in the world. My whole world seemed to turn upside down. I did not know how to deal with my father who was extremely concerned about me since his first son was supposed to carry on the

High School Friends in 1954

family tradition and take over the business.

In many ways, my grandfather was a scholar and believed a young boy needed to be guided for his development and growth. I was given plenty of liberty to do whatever I wanted. But he also emphasized that responsibility comes with freedom and that he was a strong believer in my judgment and behavior. My grandfather was a great philosopher in a sense.

I faced a rather harsh reality, after my grandfather's death. I had to explain in detail why I needed money and justify my request. My father listened carefully to my requests, but he never gave me the total amount requested. Most of the time, my request was cut down to half, and this became routine throughout my high school and college days. My father also was very harsh in dealing with any mistakes I made.

As a heart-broken teenager, I did not do well under harsh circumstances and to my deepest regret even today, I did not concentrate on my school work or preparation for the college entrance examination. It was so hard that I even thought about committing suicide many times.

After my grandfather's death, I wasted a great deal of time hanging out with my friends. And I did not prepare for the college entrance examination. During the junior year, I was attracted to a sister of my roommate, Kown, in the boarding house.

Kwon was in the second grade of middle school (8th grade) and came from Chungju, about 15 miles east of Umsong. His father had an apple orchard in town. I met his sister for the first time when Kwon's mother visited our boarding house with her daughter. She was a junior at the girl's high school in the city. We did not exchange many words, but I wrote many letters, which were never sent to her. However, I did not meet her again until she went to Ewha Women's University, and that was the last time I ever saw her.

1956 was the longest year of my life. Time did not wait for me, and I had to take the college entrance examination even though I was not prepared. The crucial time had arrived when I had to reveal that I was not prepared to take the college entrance examination. I did not tell the truth to my father, who could not understand my situation. I chose the Seoul National University law school just to say that the examination was too hard for me to do well. I did take the exam but did not even check the results of the exam. I had to tell the truth to my father and promised to spend a year in Seoul preparing for the exam. I also promised that I would do well.

In 1956, Won-heung, my next younger brother, was doing excellent middle school work in Umsong, and was asked to go to high school in Seoul since I was moving to Seoul that year. Won-heung successfully passed the entrance examination of Kyong Bok High School, and we moved to Seoul. We rented a room in the Chong-un-Dong area, where Won-heung could walk to his school. I would spend much of the daytime at the public library with Manjo, my closest friend, who also failed to go to college. While other friends were attending college, we had to spend long days preparing for it. At the end of the day, I had to go back to a small room that I shared with my younger brother.

It was the biggest news in town that I did not make it into college, and everybody in town seemed to be talking about my failure. I often thought about taking my own life during that harsh summer when most of my friends were enjoying their summer vacation. Manjo and I went swimming on a hot summer day in the Han River. The Jam-sil area was known to have a rapid current, and the width of the waterway was twice as long as the areas near the main bridge.

We both started to swim across, but Manjo gave up at the beginning. He told me later that he was scared to death. I crossed the river but had drifted a great distance, and I had to walk back a couple of miles and then cross the river one more time. There were hundreds of young swimmers, but only a few came back to the original starting point. Many of the swimmers crossed the river but took a bus to come back. I was a good swimmer who had never taken any lessons. My grandfather gave me full permission to try anything because he believed young boys needed to learn everything, even if it required some risk.

My grandfather had a strong conviction about education, but my father disagreed with his father of whom he never asked any questions. During breakfasts or dinners, I always was seated with my grandparents, and my father sat with other family members. My grandfather told everybody that a man needed to learn how to spend money in order to make money and that a man should have big ambitions and take big risks in order to succeed.

In 1950, after Seoul was recaptured by the South Korean army, we had a big store and warehouse in Shin-dang-Dong, a market section of the capital.

My grandfather had asked my father to expand our property, since our next generation would be moving to Seoul. Father did not like the risky idea and never did anything about the expansion. He closed out our Seoul operations the following year.

Until his death in 1955, my grandfather took every opportunity to harass his son for failing to expand the business in what turned out to be an exponentially growing market. After the death of my grandfather, my father did everything differently, basically just maintaining what he had, and never adapting or changing his business operations: two mills, a store, and a sizable farm. 1956 was a very difficult year for my parents witth their five sons and three daughters, as the nature of business had changed dramatically. Farming was not profitable, yet our factory depended upon farming and agricultural products.

My father quickly installed new machinery to process cotton in order to make industrial oil out of cottonseeds. It was terribly expensive to keep two children in Seoul and a few more in middle school and grade school. My father was so determined to send his children to good schools that he started selling off his assets and properties, including an apple orchard and rice fields.

He was a devoted father who did not hesitate to do what he had to for his children's education. I told him when he was in a critical condition in 1979 that I would not have sold my assets for my children's education as he did. He just smiled at me, signaling that he was glad to do it. Won-heung, who was attending Kyong Bok High School, did not know the seriousness of our troubles.

I decided to go to Korea University instead of the Seoul National University, which produced more government officials and diplomats. I did not study thoroughly for the multiple-choice examination of Seoul National, and I was encouraged to go to Korea University by my relatives, who believed I would be a political leader in the country, perhaps taking a seat in the National Assembly. The Korea University exam had essay-type questions.

I concentrated on basic information and themes of the examination subjects. In the end, I was shocked to find that I scored the second highest result among about 3,000 young applicants from all over the country. The highest scorer applied to the College of Business Administration. I applied to the College of Political Science and Economics and wanted to major in International Politics. I was the top student and was awarded scholarships. My picture was printed in the university newspaper when I went to register for the first semester.

I became a popular student once more, but because of my family's financial difficulties, I had very limited funds for an active social life. My father was brave enough to send two children to Seoul for their education in the fifties. Actually he sent the third son to Choongju and the fourth son also to Chongju later and sold off quite a large portion of cultivated land for his children's education.

3. Korea University

(Seoul)

I had wanted to go to the Military Academy or a medical school ever since I was in grade school. My physical examination for the first middle school showed I was partially color blind, which disqualified me to try for the Academy or a medical school. I did not know I could not differentiate red from green. I thought about majoring in public administration but decided to study political science instead so that I would have many opportunities to be a government official or to run for public office in the National Assembly.

Korea University Friend 1957

During the first week of March 1957, I took the entrance examination of Korea University, one of the two oldest private universities in
Korea. While other universities adopted multiple-choice and true-or-false
formats, KU's examination was essay-oriented and required in-depth
knowledge about a selected field.

There were four coeds among the freshman class in political science, and I was attracted to these young ladies. When we met for orientation, the first issue of the KU campus newspaper, in which the top three
scorers were introduced, was distributed. I became an instant celebrity
among the freshman class. Then there was an election for two class representatives, and I was elected as one of the two, the other one, Young
Chul, became my best friend until his death in 1996.

During the Japanese occupation, boys and girls were separated in all of the middle and high schools except for missionary schools and colleges. There were two famous women's universities, Ewha, and Sookmyung, and most of the female students would attend these universities as a tradition. KU, founded in 1905, had been a men's university until the establishment of the First Republic of Korea in 1948.

Syngman Rhee, himself educated at elite American universities, was elected the first president of the Republic, and began a massive reform from the Japanese to the American educational system. As one of many changes, KU opened its door to girls. However, it was only after the Korean War that female students even thought about going to coed colleges.

It surprised me to see four ladies in our 80-member political science freshman class. ES Kim, who attended one year at Ewha Women's University majoring in English literature, had switched the university and her major to political science in KU. She came from a well established family. Her father, who came down from North Korea, was a business executive, and her mother was the younger sister of a famous tenor, In-bom Lee. She lived in the Don-Am-Dong area, where many rich and famous people lived. She was like an elder sister to me and helped me a great deal with my school work and

1961 Graduation Commencement with ES Kim

Class Reunion in 1987 at Korea University

personal matters.

SJ Kim came from Won-ju Girls' High School in Kang-won province. We were on friendly terms but never got to know each other very well. She was employed by the Seoul municipal government after graduation. I met her only once after that at the 30-year class-reunion party in 1987.

JJ Lim, who graduated from Sookmyung Girls' High School, came from a family in Kang-won Province, and her brother-in-law ran for the National Assembly seat in 1958. Kwon and I were hired to be on his cam-

With Chun, Jae-ho at Class Reunion in 1987

paign staff, and we spent two weeks in Pyongchang, Kang-won province. As freshmen majoring in political science, we actually had an internship for the political election campaign. Unfortunately, he lost, but we had a wonderful time in a rural town. Lim was hired by the Korean government's diplomatic office in Los Angeles. She is now retired from her work and still lives in southern California.

HJ Cho, who had long hair like the Italian actress Malina Brady in the 1950s, was a very popular girl with a nick name of Malina among our classmates. Malina was a charming young lady, who often wrote poems. I invited her to a poetry reading session during the first month of the semester, and we became what were called campus sweethearts and a hot topic among other jealous students. We went to the movies together, but I also was studying hard in the hope that I would take the governmental examination for attorneys some time in the future.

The bar exam was the only sure way for a young Korean to move into government work, or into public office. Malina was disappointed at my lack of interest in her as I spent more time in the library or other places. Although I was interested in her, I thought I needed to work harder for my career. She maintained her interest in me during the first summer break for almost six weeks. I returned home in Umsong and tried to help my father with his factory and business. My father was not doing well with his business and was concerned about his plan to educate his eight children.

During my stay in Umsong, I received two letters from Malina. She wrote short poem-like messages on paper that was decorated with dried violet flowers. I replied to her letters with statements about what I would like to do for my career and what I thought about the future of our country. She told me later she was not terribly impressed with my nonsense letters, but she told me that she really liked me. We never used the word "love." That word, we thought, should only be used in Western movies.

When I came back to campus for the second semester sometime in August, my younger brother and I were short on money and stayed in a small rented room. I was even more determined to work hard for a good career, about which my father kept reminding me.

Malina and I remained sweethearts and the objects of admiration from many of our classmates. I was invited to her apartment, where she lived with her elder sister, and to her brother's house. I might not have been a romantic or exciting boyfriend for her, but her family seemed to like me a lot for my humor and seriousness about my career, which always came first before joining Malina or other friends in billiards or card games.

Then there was a big incident on a cold evening in late November 1957. Since I had started my KU education, I had lost touch with the high school Gang of Four. Manjo was admitted to the Business College at Seoul National University. Even though Kee-jung was admitted to a college, he was not serious about his academics. He wanted to be a movie producer or director. Man-jo and Kee-jung regularly met and played expensive games. They regularly went to dance studios and had many girlfriends with intimate relationships.

When they were told that our other friend Kwang-sook volunteered to join the air force, they thought of me and came to the KU library where I was reading a book. I could not refuse to have a farewell party for Kwang-sook. They chose a restaurant in the neighborhood of my apartment, which was shared with a friend from grade school. We all walked along the southern bank of the Sung-don River to the restaurant.

These three friends of mine had many occasions of having big dinners and a lot of drinks. It was the first time for me to have such a dinner party which I did not enjoy as much as they did. The country had a curfew from midnight to four in the morning. At around 11:30 in the night, I found out that they had left me alone. I did not have enough money to pay the bill, and I did not expect this to happen. They were much better off than I, who was struggling to survive with limited family support. It was a sizable amount, and it took me a long time to pay the bill. I never forgave my friends for that trick.

However, the worst part was not the money I owed to the restaurant. I was drunk and as I walked home I was robbed by a few beggars and gangsters. When they found out I did not have much, they beat me up pretty bad. I ran away from them with a bloody nose and blood stains on my clothes.

民参議員當選校友歡迎会記念 4293.9

By that time it was almost midnight and I knew I wouldn't be able to make it back to my apartment in time, so I stopped over at Malina's apartment, which was on the way. She was shocked by my appearance and took me to her room to give me first aid. I ended up sleeping there, but I slipped away as soon as I woke up the next morning. Although we were innocent of anything unforward, rumors flew around campus after it was discovered that I had spent the night in Malina's apartment.

Sometime after winter vacation, I spent another night in her apartment, but I was determined not to do anything that would interfere with my career goals. I also wanted to wait until I was ready to marry her. Unfortunately, that night proved to be a turning point in our relationship, which wasn't meant to be.

I still hoped Malina would help me with my coursework as a friend when I couldn't attend classes while serving military duty, but I was wrong. During eight weeks of training with the 10th Regiment of the Korean Army, I wrote Malina a few letters, but she never responded.

Then I received a letter from a classmate, CK Park, telling me that Malina was going out with another classmate, YC Kwon. I was upset when I found out what was going on, but there was nothing I could do. Malina and YC maintained their relationship until graduation, but in the end Malina married another man and YC eventually married a girl recommended by his family.

I wondered sometimes if I had maintained the relationship with Malina, what would have been my story. I would have been very vulnerable if she had been more aggressive toward me, or if I had set my priorities differently by devoting my life to a charming girl, she might not have turned her back. Anyway, I concluded that the story would have a miserable ending and I could not possibly develop my career as I wished after my graduation from university.

CK Park, who knew about my broken relationship with Malina accused me of not having feelings, and that I must be a real cold man. I never liked to be called a cold person, but I never argued with him. I told him she was not the kind of woman for me. I still think I made the right choice, but it did hurt as well. I also maintained a friendship with YC until his sudden death in 1996 at the age of 59. I thought about our relationship for many years.

In 1987, when I was a professor of journalism in the United States, I was awarded a senior Professorship to my alma mater, Korea University. There also was the 30-year class reunion party, which was a huge celebration. We met again at the party, and I greeted Malina and asked about her family. She told me that she was happily married to an advertising executive and that their daughter just graduated from Ewha Women's University. I thought I would tell her how I felt about our relationship, and that I should be the one to blame for the breakup because I did not love her with passion. However, I did not say anything. Just a few years after the class reunion in 1987, CK Park called me on the phone and told me Malina had passed away.

4. Military Service

On November 11, 1958, I was drafted to report to a military training camp at Non-san. As a 21-year-old sophomore in college, I had the option of delaying my service until I finished college and then serving 36 months in the army, or I could join the army as a college student and serve only 18 months.

I did not hesitate to accept the 18-month deal because I was planning an unusual strategy to take classes while serving my military duty.

제8352부대 I 대대

1958 in thr 10th Regiment

At the Non-san Military Training Camp, I was appointed the platoon leader for a group of 46 trainees, who were selected student soldiers from Seoul National and Korea Universities.

We formed the 8-6 Club, based on the 6th Platoon of the 8th Company in the 23rd Regiment. Members of this club became leaders in many different fields in Korean society, and they still gather on November 11, the day they were drafted, and celebrate their military experience. They had their golden anniversary in 2008.

Eight weeks of boot camp training did a lot of good for their careers. As part of the 18-month deal, we were assigned to what was called the rifle platoon in the DMZ areas. I was assigned to the first battalion headquarters of the tenth regiment of the eighth division in the Yon-chon area, where we watched movements of the North Korean army through a telescope.

My specific assignment was to S-3, operation and education, of battalion headquarters under First Lieutenant Cho, and worked on military tactical documents that were classified "secret." With strong support from headquarters personnel, I was working hard for my courses, whenever I found a few minutes from military time.

I also kept asking for family leave in order to attend classes at KU. Sometimes, dressed in military uniform, I would take exams for my courses and go straight back to my military post. It was very challenging for me to do both duties at the same time while my friends were fully enjoying campus life.

For almost two years of college life as a sophomore and a junior, I struggled to shuttle between two places, the KU campus and the military post, and managed to complete both duties.

1959

I did pretty well for my course-work with the help of ES Kim, who helped me with her notes from classes that I could not attend.

When I went back to being a full-time senior student, I had just a few courses to take and could concentrate on taking exams for a career. I passed a governmental exam n December 1960 to become a functionary under the Jang-Myun government.

I completed my compulsory military service and my college work in four years while other college friends had to serve three years in the military after graduation. My career as a government official thus began three years earlier than most of my classmates.

Uljin 1961

5. National Recon-
struction Project

(Uljin)

After passing the government examination, I was assigned to Uljin County in Kang-won province and requested to report on the 15th of January. We wore the National Development uniform and were assigned to work with local county officials for three months.

Ten National Development workers in the county were divided into five groups, and each group of two was assigned to different towns. Mr. KB Koh and I stayed in the main county office to coordinate our colleagues.

Our main task was to educate rural town folks for their community development. We asked county officials to assemble town's people during the evening hours, and we provided them with a wide range of information about the world, our country, our economy, and so on. We also had a number of question-and-answer type discussions to further their understanding.

Actually, it was even more beneficial for us to get to know people in the rural areas, who had been neglected for a long time by the Korean government. A large number of people to whom we talked spent their time gambling and drinking, and they lived in poor housing conditions, where they did not care much about their health.

The second task for us was to investigate what would be effective government projects for national development. Local officials recommended a project to develop the Baik-am hot springs, which had been known for the best quality waters. However, the place was in the rugged mountain terrain, and no highway had been built yet. Our task was to build a road first and then to design a resort area. When we drove an army jeep to the place, we discovered there was no adequate lodging or dining facilities. We reported this information and our plan to the National Development Office when we returned to Seoul.

When I went back to Korea in 2000 after my retirement from Missouri, I was amazed to find that Baik-am had become one of the nicest resort areas in Korea. There were many tourist hotels, a vacation retreat for the LG group. There was a fine highway to reach the resort. I do not know how this development took place, but I do know that we were the ones who started the whole project of which we can be very proud indeed.

Uljin also became one of the most developed towns after a nuclear power plant was constructed in the area and run by a large number of highly skilled employees. The harbor areas were booming with fishing boats and tourists. I wondered how the nuclear plant could have been built in this area without massive protests by local residents in the 1970s. I also wondered if I had done too much government propaganda for community development.

When I traveled to Uljin by train for the first time in 1961, I took a slow train to Young-ju and transferred to an even slower train to Sam-chuk. The small train was pulled by a steam locomotive and did not have enough power to ascend the Tai-baik Mountains. We were asked to walk while the train was pulled by mechanical crane to the top, and then we boarded the train again, which ran pretty fast downhill. It took more than 10 hours to travel across less than one hundred miles.

When I visited the town in 2000, it took us only three hours to drive our car from Seoul to Uljin . When we drove from Daegu to Uljin, it took less than two hours on the freeway, which was the most advanced one I had ever seen. This freeway is a straight, four-lane highway cutting through rugged mountains and over bridges connecting towns.

Bukyoung Temple 1961

We found a better way to travel from Uljin to Seoul on our way back to Seoul. We took a four-hour bus ride to reach Daegu, which was only about one hundred miles, and took an express train for four hours to travel about 250 miles.

My personal life in Uljin was memorable. When I arrived in Uljin, I was introduced by one of my friends to the Lee family, who owned and operated a tailor shop. Mrs. Lee liked me and was interested in matching me with her daughter JS Lee, who had graduated from a Seoul high school and was ready to be married off when the Lee's family found the right person.

I was invited to have dinner or drinks whenever they found me in my lodging place. Uljin was a small fishing town, where I could not find anything to do after I finished work so I was often available.. I was treated very well with many special dishes and home-made drinks and played flower cards with JS, her mother and Mr. Koh, my project partner.

As the day for us to leave town was getting closer in early March, JS invited me to go to a tourist spot with a limestone cave located about two miles west of the town, and I did not hesitate to accept the offer. I did not know, however, that this special invitation was well planned by her mother until one sunny Sunday morning when I was asked to go on a picnic with JS. They had prepared a small lunch basket.

As we walked the small country roads, both of us carried the basket that separated us instead of holding hands. We were very happy, talking about many subjects which I cannot remember now. JS told me later she liked my stories about the army training camp and DMZ experiences. She asked me about my girl-friends, but I did not tell her my story about HJ or anybody else. I just smiled back at her.

After a lengthy tour of the cave, we found a place to have our lunch. The food was wonderful especially in the company of a charming young lady. I teased her by saying that she did not sleep well the previous night preparing this lunch.

Daylight in March was not long enough for us to fully enjoy ourselves, and we rushed back to her house and had a big dinner that was prepared by her mother, who asked many questions. We told her we just enjoyed our walk in the cave and the good lunch. When I came back to my lodging place, I did not know what to do with JS.

Even though I had probably given her a very strong indication that I liked her, I was hesitant to make any promise to her yet. As the first son of the 34th generation of the Changs, I knew I should be careful about consulting my parents in such affairs. After the picnic, I avoided going to her house and traveled to other towns where other National Development workers were staying.

National Development headquarters informed us we needed to come back to Seoul sooner than originally planned. I had to leave the town without a farewell party. JS and her mother came to the bus station with a gift package of dried fish and asked me to keep them posted about my assignment. They waved their hands until the bus sped out of their sight. I did not know then that was the last time I could see them.

When we were assembled in Seoul, we were given orientation sessions and assignment slips. I was assigned to the Ministry of Agriculture and Forestry, and my working post was in the Office of Rural Development (ORD) in Daegu. I was disappointed to be assigned to Daegu, but I was told that I would not have to stay there for long and that I would be transferred to the main office soon. Actually, I stayed there for only six months.

During my stay in Daegu, I called JS on the phone a couple of times, but she was not available. It was difficult to get through a long distance phone call in Korea in 1960, and the cost of such a call was very expensive. There was the military coup by General Park, and many drastic changes in our office kept me busy day and night, so I lost touch with JS.

6. Ministry of
Agriculture
(Daegu)

Syngman Rhee, the first president of the Republic, had been in power since 1948 and was re-elected with massive voting irregularities in the March 15, 1960 election. Students from Korea University started rioting against the government on April 18, and the streets of Seoul were filled with demonstrators, who threatened to move into the office of the president. As a result, Rhee resigned the following day, and Jang Myun was elected as prime minister of the second Republic.

I was still on active duty in the 10th Regiment when the initial turmoil started and completed my duty on May 11. Prime Minister Jang, a Catholic, could not control the massive protests by various interest groups, which made unreasonable demands on the government. The whole country was in turmoil.

I was, however, one of the beneficiaries of the Jang government, which started a new policy for national development and recruited 3,000 National Development workers among college graduates. After completion of my work in Uljin, I was appointed a class 5-A official in the Daegu Office of Rural Development under the Ministry of Agriculture and Forestry.

Under the Rhee administration, there was no systematic recruitment of government employees, and a large number of officials were political appointees with temporary classifications. When I went to the Daegu office with a 5-A rank, I was assigned to the personnel section, where I, a 24-year-old bachelor, was the deputy chief. Section Chief Chin was as old as my father, and there were four others who were quite a bit older than I.

There was a big welcome party for me as I settled down in the office compound. I got along well with others. The Rural Development Office consisted of three major parts. The general administration part was responsible for personnel, accounting and purchasing. The research bureau conducted agricultural research and the extension bureau was staffed with extension workers in many different fields. My duty was to check the attendance of around 50 officials in the main office, prepare promotion and transfer of hundreds of workers in 16 counties in the province, and to keep records of the activities of our staff.

On the 16th day of May 1961, when I was almost six weeks into my job, General Park Chung Hee succeeded with his coup, declared martial law, and formed the "National Reconstruction Committee" that in effect directed the government. Under martial law, our office became a military post, where we were given orders by a communication channel in a military style. I had just come out of the military a year prior and had been used to military commands while the others were quite scared of dealing with the military.

One of the innovations of the military was to reform methods of communications between government offices by adopting military methods.

Urgent directives were sent by telephone, and all the memorandums were just like what I used to deal with when I was on military duty. I became an instant expert on official letters, and many older officials who were used to the old style, the Japanese bureaucratic style, asked for my help.

Korean typewriters were in use by some businesses, but local governments did not have them. We had to write by hand on carbon papers to duplicate. We purchased a typewriter and hired a typist, thank goodness.

Within six months, I was ordered to move to the ORD headquarters in Suwon and became a deputy in the personnel section. Now, I had to deal with 4,000 officials throughout the country and had contacts with many friends around Seoul.

I stayed in Daegu for six months, and I had become absorbed into the distinctive Kyung-sang culture with its unique southern accent and dialect. It started with my curiosity, and I tried imitating what I had heard around the office and civic center. The Korean peninsula is about the size of the state of Missouri, but there are still some regional accents that I could distinguish easily. When I moved to Suwon, some people thought I was born in Kyung-sang province.

While I had worked in Daegu, I had to travel to Suwon and Seoul quite regularly for official business or personal matters. It took the express train five hours to travel only 200 miles at that time. The train had a dining car with wider windows, through which I loved to look out at small farming villages, mountains and streams, while drinking a cold beer. Recently, Korea built a modern high-speed express train in cooperation with the makers of the French TGV, and it now takes only two hours. However, this new train moves so fast that as I look through the window, I can't seem to recollect at all what I had experienced forty years before.

Before I moved to Suwon, I found another sweetheart in Daegu by accident. The National Reconstruction Committee (NRC) ordered all the government offices to cut their staff by 15 percent, starting with employees who had a criminal record, no military service, or a record of incompetence. When we could still not reach that 15 percent, we were directed to do a capability ranking in which every official was ranked according to competency on the list of employees, and attach the list with the cut-down list.

As a deputy in the personnel section, I was responsible for drawing the list and conducting the capability ranking, which I did not believe was a fair practice. The list was made by section and rank, in which the director of the office was on top and the extension section was at the bottom. Many people thought ranking colleagues was a serious and secretive business, so they went to the restrooms or various hideouts to mark their rankings.

I did not go to such a secret place, and I was ranking the list on my desk while one of the messenger boys in our office looked on. I just ranked from the top as the best and followed the list to the bottom where, YS Kim, a 4-A extension worker for home improvement, was listed. The boy was shocked and told other boys what he had seen. Within hours, the whole ORD office knew what I had done.

I was really surprised to see the angry face of YS, who protested about my irresponsible listing and asked for the reason why she was listed at the bottom. I told her that this listing would not serve any purpose, and she did not have to worry about it. However, I knew my assurances did not help. This was how I first met Young, who has been my wife for more than 54 years.

After such a confrontation, we could not be expected to be friendly to each other, until one Sunday morning when I met her again. Under the military rule, we had to staff our office 24 hours a day. During the evening hours two male employees stayed in the office to receive telephone messages and slept in the night watch room, and female employees would come to the office on Sundays. YS came to the office to do her Sunday duty, and I also was working in my office since my living quarter was nearby. I normally did not have anything else to do.

I apologized to her about ranking her last, and asked if she would go downtown with me for a movie after five when she finished her work. We took a city bus downtown, but did not find any movie we liked. We went into a music hall where you listened to classical music while drinking tea under fairly dark illumination. I was a poor entertainer, who did not know how to please young ladies. I only bragged about my experiences in the army, which simply would not interest any woman. That was the only date I had with Young before I moved to Suwon.

May 6, 1962 at the Jeil Wedding Hall

7. Marriage

I was doing exceptionally well as I began my work for Office of Rural Development, but I was miserable in my personal life. I was still in a boarding house where I could not possibly have any privacy, nor could I rest in a family setting. There were other colleagues who stayed in the same house, and they would not leave me alone. After three months, I decided to move out.

The best excuse for moving out would be to get married. My popularity among people at ORD was very high, and I was introduced to a number of daughters from prominent families. But I had read too many western books and was determined to find the right woman for me. I did not wish to meet anyone rich or famous, or a woman with a pretty smile and charm. I wanted someone with a good mind and a kind heart. I had seen enough of pretty faces when I was in college.

Looking at myself at that time, I did not find much of what young women might be looking for. I did not have a house, unless I went back to Umsong to take over my parents' business. I only had good health, my education from Korea University and a respectable job as a government employee. I could not expect to make a young lady believe that I had a huge ambition to go abroad and obtain advanced degrees and feel my strong self-confidence in my abilities.

While I was pondering about my search for the right woman for me, I was told by my friends in the extension bureau that the national 4H contest would be held in Suwon and that Young from Kyungbuk province would come to Suwon in November 1961. I called her on the phone and asked her to meet me at her convenience during the contest. We met during lunch, and I asked her if she had anyone in her future. She said no, smiling.

All in the Family at the Wedding   May 6, 1962

After meeting Young, I was determined to move ahead with her. I looked into her personal file that was stored in my office and asked WS Shin, chief of the personnel section who had many acquaintances with senior officials in Young's province, to check her references. Mr. Shin, who graduated from the same high school about 10 years ahead of me, was like my elder brother. He told me later that "she would be too good for you."

After the holidays in January, I called her on the phone and asked to meet her and her family in Daegu sometime in February. I also asked for my parents' approval for my marriage proposal and my travel plan to Daegu in February. They were delighted to know that I finally was settling down.

So one weekend in February, I went down to Daegu and met Young's family. DK Sung, brother-in-law of Young, owner and principal of a small middle school, was in charge of handling these family matters. Young and I were the same age, 24, but it was a Korean custom that women should get married before the age of 25 while men could be much older, as they had to complete college and military service for three years. I do not remember what I said to her and her family, but it was understood by both sides that I had proposed to marry Young.

Honeymoon in Busan 1962

As a tradition, her family needed to visit my parents to consult about the wedding. Young's mother and her cousin went to Umsong and met my parents while Young and I were not present. As a matter of fact I was asked to be at one of the military training camps for one week training as a reserve soldier during their visit. I found out at the military training camp that both parties agreed to have a wedding in May in Daegu.

According to Korean wedding tradition, the groom's family needed to send a box of gifts before the wedding day. The contents of the box vary from region to region. The custom of the Kyungsang area was to fill the box with lavish jewelry, clothing, makeup kits, and money and so on while the Chungchong area prepared only red and blue silk textiles for the bride. I had what my parents prepared.

This gift box should be carried by friends of the groom, and the bride's family should provide ceremonial dinner, drinks and expenses. I asked my college friend YC to deliver the box in the evening before the wedding day, May 6, 1962. After the delivery, I invited all of my friends from Seoul who would come to the wedding and friends of Young to a Chinese restaurant for a banquet.

It was a big party with lavish dishes and heavy partaking of very expensive Chinese liquor. A wedding reception was planned after the ceremony, but the newlyweds were to leave for their honeymoon after the reception. This type of banquet before the wedding was necessary for the young people to get to know each other. It was a prenuptial party.

Young and her family had been members of the Anglican Church, and they asked to have a church wedding. But the church firmly rejected this on the basis of the church policy that it does not support members marrying non-members. Our wedding ceremony was held in the First Wedding Hall that used to be a city-owned botanical garden.

KS Moon, principal of the Kyungbok High School, conducted the ceremony which took more than an hour, so the bride and the groom had to stand on the podium for a long time. There were a few congratulatory remarks by distinguished guests, one friend of the bride and another one from the groom's friends. JH Shin, a member of 8-6 Club, intentionally spoke way too long to harass me. After more than 47 years, we still chuckle about what he tried to do at my wedding. I promised him that I would do the same, but I was already in the States when he had his wedding.

HY Park who was working in the Office of Railroad Transportation arranged our travel in an express train and reserved our honeymoon room in s Busan tourist hotel, which was owned and managed by his office. HY and three other friends followed us to the honeymoon hotel and gave us friendly ribbings.

On the four o'clock train to Busan, we were accompanied by four members of 8-6 Club. When we arrived at Busan station, a big 1959 Chevrolet Caprice sedan, a so-called 'weeping eyes,' was waiting to take us honeymooners to the tourist hotel in Haeundae. We stayed in the luxury Room, # 205, with the help of HY Park.

After the wedding, we as a couple hurried to move into a rented part of a house with two bedrooms, a kitchen and wooden floored family room. Won-heung occupied the small bedroom and he commuted to school by train. Young resigned from her work in Daegu and became a housewife. She must have been bored to death after working full time for many years for the government with a respectable rank and salary.

We were pursuing the possibility of getting her position back in a nearby county. It seemed possible when some female extension workers in nearby counties were getting married and resigned their positions. I repeatedly explored this possibility with my chief and head of the Home Improvement department, who agreed to help when such an opportunity arose.

Before too long, a position in the main office of the Home Improvement department was open. However, a big obstacle was the rule that a husband and wife should not be allowed to work in the same building. There was no such case, so I processed appointment papers and obtained the necessary signatures of the officials concerned except for the signature of the Director-General Dr. Chung. I waited for the right moment for Dr. Chung to sign the document and obtained his signature without any questions asked.

Young started working as an extension officer in the same building. It was not long before the secret leaked by jealous co-workers, and everybody seemed to know what had happened. When Dr. Chung was informed about the appointment, I was told that he was very upset and that he ordered us separated when the right time came. I did not agree with the policy, but I was not the Director-general.

Young was well received by the head of the department and her colleagues, with whom she had been associated for many years. It was hard to find an excuse to punish her. About six months later, I was ordered by the new Director-General Dr. Hyun to be transferred to the Institute of Agricultural Technologies which was located in a different building in the same compound.

In March 1965, Susan and I were shopping around the city market and a number of young ladies who were employees of restaurants greeted us. I noticed a sign of suspicion on Susan's face. When we came back to our apartment, Susan dutifully reported to her mother what she had seen. Young and I laughed and laughed about the instinct of women that was already there when they were so young.

Anthony was born on April 30, 1965, and my parents were delighted to have the first son of the next generation of the Chang family. By then I had received a number of university acceptances. I received congratulations for my admissions to U.S. schools and was expected to leave the country around the summer of 1965.

8. Office of Rural Development

(Suwon)

I had been excited about moving to Suwon where I could plan ahead for my career. I moved into a boarding house just outside of the main building of the Office of Rural Development, but I had to work in my office all the time except for sleeping in my room and early breakfast at the boarding house.

ORD was strongly supported by the military government. General Park, who became the president of the Third Republic, was determined to develop agricultural innovations. During the early stage of the military government, a colonel in uniform was assigned as the Deputy Director General to supervise our operations.

Colonel CR Choi was a scary figure who always had his right hand on his handgun holster when he visited our office. He did not say much, nor did he ask any questions. He just wanted to hear our reports on what we were doing at that time.

綠色革命成就

ORD Visit with Chancellor Uehling 1979

The military government had adopted six revolutionary pledges, which it ordered everybody to commit to memory, including students, government employees, civilians, and so on. When we started the day at 8 o'clock in the morning, we all had to assemble together and recite the pledges in military style. But most of the ORD officials did not memorize these six pledges.

We were inspected repeatedly by a group of military personnel to see how we were following their directives. On one Monday morning, inspectors in military uniforms arrived and occupied the office of the Director-General. They requested senior staff members to be present. When all senior directors were assembled, the head of inspectors asked if anyone in the office could recite the pledges by memory.

When he did not find anyone, he asked to bring in one who could do it. The director-general thought I should be able to handle it since I was one of the youngest just out of college. I was asked to come to his office, which was on the second floor. When I opened the door, the general screamed at me, ordering me to recite the pledges. I could not do it. I did not think the revolutionary pledges were for us professional employees of the government.

1962: ORD Executive Officers

Even so, I was given the task of expanding the organization and getting approval from the National Reconstruction Committee in Seoul. The expansion was to establish our offices of extension at the county level, and the head of extension workers was classed 3-A, the same level as a county chief. Dr. Chung, Director-General of ORD who was educated at the University of Wisconsin, was supported by the United States Operation Mission (USOM), which funded the major costs of buildings and equipment for 165 extension offices. I worked most of the time in Seoul for three months for the approval from the government during the reorganization period.

After the completion of the expansion, I was given the task of recruiting 3,000 extension workers through an open and fair examination of agricultural subjects. The whole country welcomed President Park, who announced that national reconstruction should start at the grassroots level of farmers and agricultural industry. Therefore, ORD was reorganized, recruiting 3,000 government officials. It was a time when the rate of unemployment was very high, and the economy of the country was much worse than North Korea's.

I rented the whole campus of the college of agriculture and forestry at Seoul National University, which was within walking distance from our office. There were about 15,000 qualified applicants. For the examination, we needed to collect confidential questions from professors and experts, have the questions designed by a five-member committee, who were secluded in an undisclosed location, and to print 15,000 copies of the exam papers. It was a massive undertaking, but we handled it successfully, and I was praised by everybody involved.

The United Nations Korean Soil Fertility Project:

Dr. Hyun explained to me that my transfer was necessary for the Institute of Agricultural Technologies, which was proposing a joint project with the United Nations Special Fund. For the development of the project, an administrative officer who could manage English was needed, and I was the one selected. I was disappointed to move down to the branch organization, but as it turned out, the transfer helped me pursue my goal of going to the States for further education.

The United Nations Korean Soil Fertility Project (UNKSOF) was to measure the quality of farming soils and develop an overall map and statistics of the Korean farmland. The United Nations designated the Food and Agriculture Organization (FAO) in Rome to work with the Korean government. FAO was to bring three experts and equipment, and the Korean government was to provide all the necessary manpower and expenses. The project was to be completed in five years, and then the Korean government would take over the project after its completion.

In 1963, the Korean government did not have foreign currencies to bring in international experts and to buy expensive equipment. It was an exciting project for the Korean government. FAO experts had arrived. Dr. George Vermaat (Dutch) was an agronomist and project co-manager. Mr. Prasad (Indian) was a statistician, and Antonio Becerra Lawrence (Spanish) was the administrative officer, who also was my counterpart for the project.

I was also appointed as the disbursing officer who had to sign every voucher and check. All of our accounting and administrative documents were in English, and I had to hire two secretaries and a typist for my office. I also hired three clerks for our work, brought in from the Institute of Agricultural Technologies.

We imported three cars; a Toyota Crown Station Wagon, a four-wheel drive Land Cruiser and a jeep. For the collection of soil samples throughout the country, we imported 50 motorcycles. The project was running smoothly, and I enjoyed one motorcycle assigned to me. I used it to go to the office, and rode it to Seoul when no other vehicle was available.

I was also provided a government-owned housing unit, which had bigger space than our rented one. Young resumed her work after a month's leave when Susan was born on March 21, 1963 and later Anthony on April 30, 1965. We had to hire a nanny from my hometown and Won-heung stayed with us until his graduation from Seoul National University.

When we received 50 motorcycles, we delivered five to each province. It was late October when Becerra and I decided to go down to Kyungbuk and Kyungnam provinces with 10 motorcycles. Becerra and his wife had been asking to travel across the countryside of the peninsula and Young wanted to visit her mother with two-year-old Susan. The Toyota Land Cruiser had plenty of space for a driver and five passengers and enough power to pull a loaded trailer.

We left Suwon for Daegu around 10 o'clock in the morning, but it took us all day to drive 200 miles to Daegu just in time to have dinner with the provincial people. There was no freeway at that time, and it took us longer than expected. Young and Susan stayed with grandmother a couple of days while Becerra, his wife, and I went down to Jinjoo for the delivery of motorcycles to Kyungnam province.

When I came back to Daegu and picked up Young and Susan, we had a big lunch at a local restaurant. After an early lunch, we left Daegu for our long travel to Suwon. We had many drivers in addition to Mr. Lee, the official driver. Becerra and I also had our driver's licenses. During our trip, we took turns driving the car.

When we stopped over in Kimchon for coffee and tea, Becerra was in a good mood and volunteered to drive the car, and nobody objected. However, within an hour, we had a terrible accident. Our car could not avoid a young man on a bicycle. He was drunk and was killed. We carried the body to a local police station, since we could not find a hospital in a small rural town. I had to ask for police protection for United Nations diplomatic personnel. We were escorted to the Youngdong police headquarters before masses of villagers swarmed to protest.

Becerra did not use his diplomatic privilege and pleaded guilty to a manslaughter charge. He promised to accept whatever punishment was given and to provide compensation to the family. The accident was reported on a radio news show, in which the reporter mentioned my name as the driver of the vehicle. The police needed to prepare the accident report, and there was no policeman who could use English or Spanish to ask questions of Becerra. I was appointed as an official translator. It took us many hours to complete the report.

When we arrived in Suwon, I had to report the trip in detail to the director-general and his staff, who were not happy about everything I did. Becerra did his part with the offices of FAO and the United Nations. The trial was held in absentia, and the court gave a suspended sentence on condition that the family of the deceased would accept the compensation amount.

I was then sent to the family of the deceased to negotiate the compensation. It was one of the most difficult things I have had to do in my whole life. Representatives of the family were angry but demanded a reasonable amount of compensation to purchase farmland of about one acre for family support and the cost of funeral expenses.

After consulting with Becerra, I agreed to meet the demand. And I had to deliver a sack full of cash to the family members, who took many hours to count. Becerra, a Catholic, took the accident hard and requested to return to Rome. But he stayed in Korea until the end of the project.

Becerra became a closer friend to me after the accident, and we exchanged our thoughts about life and work. Becerra who knew of my long-range plan to go to the United States encouraged me strongly to pursue my goal. He also wanted to help me with the plan. I already had a family with young Susan and my pregnant wife, and I did not have much savings. It was unthinkable for an ordinary person like me to try such an adventure.

I started applications for admission to graduate programs at a few journalism schools. I wanted to study journalism, which was not my undergraduate major, but I was hooked by this area of study. Becerra edited my application materials and helped me to obtain recommendation letters from high ranking officials of the United Nations.

I also had to study for the examination by the Korean Ministry of Foreign affairs in order to get a permit to study abroad. The examination covered only two subjects: English and Korean history. I did not worry about my English, but I had to study and prepare for the history exam, which I last dealt with when I was in high school.

Once I had decided to resign from my post, and leave the country, I pretty much transferred my workload to Oh who did not speak much English but was eager to take over. I even had free time to take three-year old Susan to the city markets. She loved to ride on the motorcycle. There were few cars or motorcycles on the streets of Suwon in 1965, and we were quite free and safe to cruise around the city.

I had already attended a number of farewell parties and was expected to leave the country. I had a hard time explaining what had happened to all of the well-wishers for my study. I finally passed the exam in October and started to prepare for my trip to the States. There were not too many choices of transportation for me. Airfare across the Pacific was $430, which was a large amount for ordinary Korean folks. My father had given me the money six months before, but I had to use some of it for other purposes.

The Ministry of Foreign Affairs suggested that I take one of the cargo ships that regularly crossed the ocean. I found one with the fare of $230.00. The ship would leave on March 17 and arrive in Vancouver, Washington, after 19 days. I decided to take it.

I also requested Young's transfer to an office nearby Daegu so that she and our two children could stay with our children's grandparents for one or more years until I could bring them to the States. When I was in the main office, people in the Kyungbuk provincial office were friendly to us. But they did not help us much when they knew I already had left for the States. Young had a very tough year with her office.

Part II
American Education

1.   Crossing the Pacific

It was windy and cold in the morning of March 19, 1966 when our family took a train from Daegu to Busan. For two hours, we did not talk much at all. We were in deep thoughts about the dramatic change for our family.

I did not know much about America or American education. I did not have any close friends in the land of opportunity. I had enormous anxiety about my adventure. I was about to leave my wife and two young children in Korea. We did not have any savings, but Young would continue working for the government to support the family. She also was scared to face the challenge. Our two children, Susan, 3, and Anthony, just about a year and a half, could not comprehend the situation but felt the heavy mood of their parents. They did not get to enjoy the train ride that they had wished to have so many times.

Pacific Ocean

When we arrived at the Busan station, we felt our time of separation getting closer and did not know when we would meet again. I even thought about cancelling the whole plan while looking at our two innocent children. The old Busan railroad station was surrounded by many good restaurants. We chose one near the customs area, where I was supposed to check in around 3 o'clock in the afternoon. We ordered many dishes, but we were not interested in them. I was trying hard to convince them that all of us were going to be reunited really soon after a year of my stay in the States. However, they as well as I knew that nothing was certain for our future.

Around 2 o'clock, I checked into the custom area and bade farewell to my family. They could watch me going through the check point and boarding a small ferry boat to get on the Jinduck, which anchored about a mile from the harbor. We kept waving our hands until we could not see each other anymore. When Anthony and Susan were asked where their dad went, they would answer, "My dad went into the water."

The Jinduck (named after an Empress of the Shilla Dynasty around the 10th century) slowly moved out of the Busan harbor around 9 o'clock in the evening. She had been built by the Germans around 1955 and was purchased by the Korea Maritime Corp in 1965.

Astoria, Oregon

When we arrived at the Busan station, we felt our time of separation getting closer and did not know when we would meet again. I even thought about cancelling the whole plan while looking at our two innocent children. The old Busan railroad station was surrounded by many good restaurants. We chose one near the customs area, where I was supposed to check in around 3 o'clock in the afternoon. We ordered many dishes, but we were not interested in them. I was trying hard to convince them that all of us were going to be reunited really soon after a year of my stay in the States. However, they as well as I knew that nothing was certain for our future.

Around 2 o'clock, I checked into the custom area and bade farewell to my family. They could watch me going through the check point and boarding a small ferry boat to get on the Jinduck, which anchored about a mile from the harbor. We kept waving our hands until we could not see each other anymore. When Anthony and Susan were asked where their dad went, they would answer, "My dad went into the water."

The Jinduck was operated by about 39 crew members. The captain was Captain Nam, who had graduated from the Korea Maritime College around 1950. The crew consisted of three navigation officers, a chief engineer, three other engineers, a communication officer, a secretary and about 29 other crew members. The cargo ship also has six guest rooms. I was not the only one who could not afford airfare. Two other young men were literally in the same boat as me, and we became fast friends.

Three of us young students were assigned to guest rooms and treated like their officers, with whom we could dine lavishly compared with other crew members. During the 19-day journey across the Pacific, we were treated well and allowed to see every corner of the ship. We were also taught many interesting navigation techniques.

We became good friends with the people who worked in the recreation room, which was called "the Salon." Three young crew members were assigned to help the captain and officers. I tried to read books on journalism during the journey, but my mind was wondering about the uncertain future: My dear wife and two children were thousands of miles away and I was going to study journalism in an American university. I was accompanied by the three young men in the salon; they listened to my stories, and moreover, they played classical music and taught me how to ballroom dance.

The Pacific was named after calm and peaceful water, but the ocean was very rough in March. I became seasick while I was already homesick after five days, and we were in the middle of the ocean. The crew suggested I should go out on to the deck and get some fresh air. However, damp and windy air in the middle of the Pacific did not help me at all. After a 16-day journey from Japan, I was told we were about to see the North American continent. Finally, we approached Astoria, the entrance of the Columbia River, our final stopover. My destination was Vancouver, Washington, located on the banks of the Columbia River. I was exhausted and sick after being in a constantly moving boat on water. Even some crew members were excited about the scenery along the Columbia River. I was not interested in the beauty and the wonder of nature. But picturesquely beautiful houses on the bank and on mountain cliffs were so impressive that I, for a long time, still dream about the trip.

My desire to go to America had been motivated and encouraged by KI Koh, elder brother of Kwangsook, my classmate from high school. Brother Koh was preparing his trip to the U.S.A. in 1953 when the Korean War was stopped with a ceasefire agreement. I was a 9th grader then. Since my high school and Korea University days, I had been preparing for my adventure to this land of opportunity.

I had worked hard to master the English language and volunteered to join the Korean army. There were three basic requirements for a young man who wanted to study abroad during the Syngman Rhee government. First they needed to pass government examinations in two subjects: English and Korean history. Secondly, they must have served in the Korean military for a determined period of time, and finally, they needed a sponsor, who could pay for school expenses.

I had served in the Korean army when I was in college and also met this second requirement. My English skills were excellent among my Korean friends. I also had passed the Korean government placement exam for the Ministry of Foreign Affairs during the Jang Myun administration. And I was assigned a job in the Ministry of

Agricultural Forestry right before my graduation with a B.A. degree in Political Science. It was because of my English skills I was transferred to the United Nation Special Fund Program on Soil Fertility Project.

The final requirement of financial support was the most difficult one. I could not save any money as I worked for the Korean government even as a high ranking officer. I was already married and had two children by 1965, when I was planning to leave Korea. And I could not expect any help from my parents, who already had financial difficulties sending their four children to college.

The Korean government allowed me to exchange only $50 for my education in the United States. I had a $100 bill, given me by Francis Lee, husband of Young's younger sister who worked as an architect in a U.S. military unit in Daegu. The total funds for my living in the U.S. was that $150. It was early March of 1966 when a 29-year-old young man full of energy and ambition started his adventure.

I had applied for graduate admissions at a number of well-known American universities such as Northwestern, Stanford, Wisconsin and the University of Oregon. I quickly found that the University of Oregon was the least expensive in tuition, and the school promised some financial support based on my ability to work for the school.

In 1965, the University of Oregon was one of the two professionally oriented journalism schools on the West Coast. The other one was the University of Southern California, where I would later enroll for my Master's degree. Many good recommendation letters from colleagues in the United Nations special fund project and teachers from the Korea University helped me receive a tuition waiver and a possible assistantship. The University of Oregon was a perfect match for my need. I did not even try to pursue other schools.

2. Gresham, Oregon

Park's Nursery

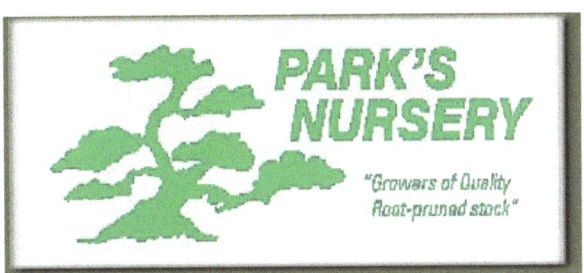

After 19 torturous days to cross the Pacific, we finally reached the Vancouver harbor. It was a beautiful spring day, when the Rev. Kim of the Portland Korean Church drove his station wagon to the harbor and invited three students to dinner at his church. I noticed that the Rev. Kim's car had the Korean flag painted on its door.

My immediate needs were to find a place to stay until August when the new school year would start and to find work to save money for my education. Rev. Kim was very kind to help me find both a place to work and to stay. He had some ideas and started calling his friends. He asked me whether I would work for a nursery farmer. I did not hesitate for a moment to accept the offer.

Since the Jinduck was anchoring three days in the Vancouver port, I could stay in my room on the ship for that time. The Rev. Kim came to us every morning to help me and other crew for our personal needs like shopping and sightseeing. After three more days on the ship, I moved to Harry Park's Nursery in Gresham, the nursery farmer for whom I was to work, located 19 miles east of Portland. Gresham was a small town of about 20,000 It has since became a suburb of Portland.

Harry was a second generation Korean immigrant, whose parents immigrated to Hawaii at the turn of this century. Harry, who spoke a few Korean words, married a Korean in 1955, and they had three boys and a girl. I was told by Harry that the farm had been started with his father in 1947.

After retirement from her work for a banking business in Korea, Harry's mother-in-law came to live with the family in a newly built large house, where I became a roommate with his oldest son, Tom, a first grader.

They owned about 40 acres of land, where they grew landscaping trees and Scotch Pines for Christmas. Harry was a hard-working farmer who got up before sunrise and stayed in the field until sunset. His children were too young to help. His wife, Rocky, and Grandma helped him seeding and transplanting trees, but they could not operate farm machinery such as tractors.

My main job was to help him operate that machinery. I was promised one dollar an hour, and lived there like a family member. Summer months in Oregon west of the mountains were very dry with lots of sunshine. The weather was perfect for growing trees if we supplied water manually. Before sunset everyday, Harry and I moved irrigation pipes from one place to another to water trees. The one hard and difficult job was to dig out trees to transport them to clients. Since they treated me as a member of the family, I went to church or parties or town together with them.

One time we went to the west coast to collect mussels and seaweed and came back with many bags. We cleaned them and stored them in the freezer to be used for many months. Harry also was an insurance agent, and he helped neighboring Korean as well as American families with their insurance and other problems.

Every Friday night, folks from five or six Korean families in the Gresham area came to Harry's house to play cards and enjoy each other's company. They asked me to join them and even insisted that they would teach me how to play. It was a nickel and dime game for fun, not really gambling. I repeatedly declined and sometimes watched their game, or I went into my room to read books. When they offered me a drink of beer or a cigarette, I always said "no" without hesitation, but I used to drink beer and liquor and smoke heavily until I moved to Harry's farm.

On the hot summer evenings, I was dying to have a cold beer and smoke cigarettes. However, I had to refrain from the fun. I had come to the States to get my doctoral degree, and I was determined to try my best to accomplish that goal and not to do anything that might jeopardize it.

Grandma was like my mother, who watched over me carefully and took care of all of my needs. She somehow thought I might drink and smoke but did not encourage me to develop a "bad habit." She literally cried when she found out about my bad habits after I went to the University and visited the family during one weekend. That weekend in September, I visited Harry's farm with a couple of Korean friends. When we arrived on the farm, I was smoking cigarettes and took a can of beer without thinking what I used to do earlier on the farm. Grandma was watching me and started crying.

Grandma did not speak much English, and her grandchildren did not speak Korean at all. She therefore did not spend too much time with her grandchildren. She did, however, often go to the Greyhound Race Track in Portland. The track was exactly like a horse race track, except that greyhounds were running to catch a robot rabbit. She spent some time and money on gambling, and I was repeatedly asked to go with her to help read statistics of the greyhounds.

I enjoyed my stay on Harry's nursery farm as I felt like a member of the family, who would care for one another. It was a great learning experience for me who had left home to explore the world without my family. It also was my first encounter with an American family and society. I admired the Parks and am still grateful for what they had done for me.

The three months of work and life with the Parks went by quickly. I then went down to Eugene to register for the first term at the University of Oregon. I was admitted as a graduate student, but I needed to take some junior level courses in journalism. I also signed up to stay in a dormitory for the first term. It cost me more to stay in the dorm than in a rented room like other Korean students, but I was dying to have a real campus life, which I had not been able to have at Korea University.

I felt like a teenager who was leaving his family to go to college when I started packing my stuff. I did not have much to pack in the aluminum trunk that was used to deliver our wedding gifts. Grandma gave me a down-filled winter overcoat and told me I needed a heavy coat at night on campus. I wore it all the time when weather got chilly in the night and felt her love. I wore the lucky jacket throughout my six years on campuses until I finished my doctoral degree.

The University of Oregom 1966

3. Eugene, Oregon: Univ. of Oregon
Bachelor of Arts in Journalism

As a 29-year-old graduate student, I was a young and energetic man. The campus life I had been dreaming about for a long time finally became a reality. But it would begin with hard training for a journalist rather than a purely enjoyable experience.

My language skills were good enough for me to be elected the Social Chairman of the Bean Hall Dormitory. Some Korean female students thought I was very attractive and repeatedly asked for dates. I declined by saying I was already married and the father of two children, which they did not believe. I had to show my family pictures to convince them. All but one student did not change her mind, and persisted in chasing me. It was very flattering, but a bit uncomfortable.

Students Picnic at Corvallis 1966

I, however, was miserable in my first reporting class. It started with the reporting of a traffic accident, which was filmed and shown to us in the class for 10 minutes. Then we were asked to write a report for a newspaper.

First, I could not get as many facts in the given time, as the other students, who were Americans. My typing skill on the old manual Royal typewriter was also way below average. I could not finish the story in the 50 minutes of the class time. Professor Halverson sometimes gave me extra minutes, but I was not doing very well.

Professor Halverson, reporting class instructor, asked me to go with him to his office after a class and suggested that I read American newspapers carefully and study how reports were written. Our reporting lectures covered a dozen different topics that were in the syllabus. I spent an enormous amount of time memorizing many types of reports like obituaries, town meetings, school board meetings, court reporting and so on. All I had to get was the right names of the persons involved and other facts of the topic. I passed the first reporting class, and the professor was really happy with my progress.

The University of Oregon

One of the toughest assignments was to report on a Richard Nixon campaign speech in town sometime in the fall of 1967. We went to the place, heard the speech and wrote our report before midnight of the day. I was surprisingly awarded an A for my story. I had read almost every speech Nixon did in different towns and made notes for different subjects. When I went to Nixon's speech, I needed to check out which topic he was talking about and already had ideas about which topic should be on the top and what the headline should be.

Another class was on the History of American Journalism taught by Professor Warren Price, a well-known journalism historian. I was miserable trying to memorize strange names of pioneers of American journalism. My answers to exam questions had many misspellings in their names, and I was punished dearly for them. Sometimes I still have nightmares trying to spell out correct names of my students and friends.

I had just enough money to cover one term in the dormitory, but money was running out faster than I had expected. Most of the Korean students were doing part-time work in restaurants as dishwashers in the evening. My close friend Min was working in the student union where many of his friends had coffee or sodas. I became desperate trying to find work.

I found an ad for janitors in the local newspaper. It was for the Von Marche department store. I applied and was hired after an aptitude test. It was a full-time job, but work hours were in the evening all the way to two o'clock in the morning. The job required too many hours for a full-time student, but it paid good money. Min was getting one dollar an hour at the University, but I was getting $1.75 an hour in 1966.

I checked in at 5 or 9 in the evening while the store was still open, went down to the basement, where a gas furnace was situated, and burned used wooden or paper boxes for packing. We did not have any idea of recycling in 1966 and burned good paper boxes that could have been reused or recycled. I would hang my notes on the side of the furnace and read aloud while I was feeding boxes into the furnace. Luckily, nobody would come down to the area, which was filled with smoke, heat and dust.

Around 11 at night we took a half hour break in the basement restaurant, where the kitchen workers always stored cakes or pies for us. I really enjoyed chatting with other janitors and I learned more about America society from a different segment. I worked as a box-burner until I was promoted to the assistant superintendent position and given a set of keys to the store. As I moved up to a supervisory position, my work for the department store had become easier, and I did not have any difficulty to keep up with my course work.

I also had the chance to buy a car from my roommate, who had come down from Alaska and did not need the car anymore. The vehicle was a 1954 Ford, a beat-up sedan, and I paid only $45 for it. The automobile ran well enough to get me to my work and to help other students when they had to move. Few Korean students had a car in 1966.

When I finished my shift around two in the morning, I usually went to the lounge area to catch up with my course work, and ended up sleeping in the lounge a number of nights. There were other students who would come to the lounge for their studies, either because their roommates brought their dates to the dormitory room or some other reason. I just did not want to wake up my roommate at two o'clock in the morning.

Few Korean students knew what I was doing at night, and they thought I came from a rich family because I could afford a car while I was at the university. I was, however, worrying a lot since I could not save enough to bring my wife and children to Oregon. I decided to move into a one-room apartment when the second term started in January.

The International Student Office helped students from abroad. One of the many programs was a friendship family arrangement. My host family was Mr. William Kunkle, He was an insurance adjuster while he was working as a freelance photographer. He was amazed to find a Korean student studying journalism, an area he thought would have been too hard because of the language.

I was invited to their home on many Sundays when our dorm did not serve meals. For Thanksgiving dinner, they invited me and a number of their relatives, and we all enjoyed a big 20-pound turkey. I also was invited to their church and asked to tell my stories to a group of high school kids. When I spoke about my family in the church, many kids asked me why I did not bring them to Oregon. I responded that there were two things I did not have; I did not have enough money for their travel and living in Oregon, and I needed a financial affidavit signed by an American for their travel. Mr. Kunkle offered to sign the financial affidavit for my family. He also suggested I get a bank loan for the expenses, since he knew I was working for Von Marche. I was extremely grateful for the support of Mr. Kunkle, and started invitation process.

At the end of the first term before Christmas, I moved into a two-story house owned by Mrs. Myrtle McRae, who had retired from teaching. The house was a big old one with an attic-type bedroom upstairs and three bedrooms on the ground level. She used only one big bedroom, and rented three rooms to Korean students. Young Soo Yae, a student in English literature, completed his doctoral degree, taught many years in Korean universities, retired and became an evangelical minister. JW Yoon, a graduate student in biochemistry, finished his doctoral degree in Oregon. He worked as a prominent researcher for the National Institute of Health for a long time. I was the third.

The house was on 16th Street, just five blocks from the campus. I moved into a room on the second floor. Mrs. McRae volunteered to clean our rooms occasionally and treated us like her own children. We all shared one kitchen and one small refrigerator, which was filled with our stuff. She invited us to many meals, which we never liked that much since her dishes were mostly leftovers. She had gone through the Great Depression and told us no food should be wasted.

She did not see me much or know me that well since I had been working full time in the evenings. One Sunday morning, I was reading textbooks and heard her complaining that the boy who used to mow her lawn was not coming to work for her. I told her I would be more than happy to do the job. I found out that the lawnmower did not have a power-engine and pushing it was hard work. The boy was, understandably, not eager to come to work for the two dollars.

When Mrs. McRae came back from her church service, she was delighted to find the nicely shaved grass and wanted to pay me two dollars. I told her I could not take money for the work for my own house, even though I was only renting a room. She really liked my sincerity. I took care of her grass until I moved out of the house.

She liked me a lot when she found out that I was a full-time student and a full-time employee of a department store. She was watching me carefully and tried helping me any way she could. When I was finally following through on Mr. Kunkle's suggestion and going to get a bank loan for Young's airfare of $450, she wrote me a check for the amount and told me to pay it back when I was ready. I was going to write a receipt, but she said that was not needed. During the summer vacation, I worked hard for three months and paid back her money. My family and I could not fully express how grateful we were for her kindness and trust.

As the end of the school year was coming closer, many Korean students were getting ready to go to the Lake Tahoe casino/resort area for summer jobs. I decided to go, too, and planned to drive. I had two female students as passengers in the old car, which had some difficulty climbing up the 14,000 feet mountain, but it made it. When we arrived at the Washoe County office, we were fingerprinted, since we were going to work in casinos.

During the middle of May, the casinos were gearing up for the big summer, and they loved students working during the summer months. I was hired as a bar boy in the CalNeva casino owned by Frank Sinatra at that time. The casino was built on the border line between California and Nevada. On the Californian side, the resort hotel was built and the casino was on the Nevada side.

CalNeva Resort and Casino

I was assigned to work in a dug-out bar, built in front of the stage, on which the Kirbystone Brothers were performing loud rock music. My job as a bar boy was to assist professional bartenders by washing glasses and filling the ice boxes. There were three shows a night and it was packed with gamblers who drank. However, the worst part of my job was to hear the same loud music three times a night. When the drummer beat the electronic drum hard, I felt like he was beating me up.

I worked the so-called graveyard shift from eight in the evening to four the next morning. After the final midnight show, the bar was fairly slow with just a few gamblers, who always bragged about how much they lost or won. I was given a break at which time I would go to the main kitchen to have my New York steak sandwich. We were allowed to have only sandwiches, but the chefs were very nice to students. We were also supplied by the chefs with expensive drinks in soda cups.

Seven students from Oregon shared a small apartment with two bedrooms. We had different shifts and we could sleep on a bed when it was not occupied. I was so tired at four in the morning that I could sleep anywhere on a sofa or even on the floor. After about three hours of sleep, I went to work for my second job as a laundry man for a motel in the area from eight in the morning till four in the afternoon. Most of us worked two jobs.

Lake Tahoe Resorts

Working the two jobs for three months meant I could save about $3,000 which was enough for school for a whole year. It was hard for everybody. I was so exhausted that one day I was looking for a sock while I was holding the sock in my hand. Min, my close friend for a long time, saw what I was doing and screamed "I hope he is not losing his mind."

We, of course, did not have any opportunity to spend money while working two jobs. But there were a few friends who gambled and never came back to the campus after the summer. I had to work extra hard to save money for my wife's travel expenses from Korea.

I sent Young the money. She got the paperwork done and tele-grammed me that she was arriving in San Francisco on the fifth day of August, just about two weeks before our work was completed in the casino. It was a four-hour drive on winding mountain highways to the airport. When I arrived there, the BOAC flight she was going to take had been canceled. And I had to drive back another four hours with a heart broken from disappointment. We did not have the luxury of telephone service as we do now. I had to wait another four days to go back to the airport to pick her up.

All my friends welcomed her and said we were having our second honeymoon at Lake Tahoe. She helped us with cleaning the apartment and doing everyone's laundry in return for the favor of having one bedroom for us only. For the first time, I went down to the South Shore, where more popular casinos and resort settings were located. However, I had to continue what I was doing until the last day of my job.

When we were driving back to Eugene, Oregon, Young and I felt very guilty about Susan and Anthony, who were left behind with their grand-mother in Daegu. We agreed to bring them to Oregon as soon as possible, but we knew it was not going to be easy.

Young and I moved into one of many apartments, which were built to accommodate the large number of married students, who were coming back to school with their GI support after the end of WWII. It was a wooden struc-ture two-bedroom unit, which cost us only $40 a month. We had some breathing room in our apartment and even invited Mrs. McRae over for din-ner. We could not thank her enough for her generosity which helped Young come to the States.

Young started her work as a baby sitter for two boys of a Taiwanese couple who were both doctoral students and lived nearby. The two boys liked Young very much, and they did not want to leave and often stayed with us for supper. With the savings from Lake Tahoe and Young's work, I was able to quit my job at the department store and concentrate fully on my course work.

As I finishing my second BA degree in two years, I was permitted to stay on for a Master's degree. But then we were shocked to find that Young was pregnant. We already had two children whom we needed to bring to the States, and we really could not afford to have another child. But that was fate.

After receiving my BA in journalism in May, we decided to go to Los Angeles where I hoped to go to the University of Southern California even-tually and to prepare for our third child who was expected to be born in Au-gust. We also hoped to send for Susan and Anthony to have all our family together in Los Angeles. We packed everything in our second car, a 1959 Chevrolet sedan, the same kind, we had ridden in during our honeymoon in Korea in 1962. We drove down to San Francisco, where we played for one day, and arrived in Los Angeles on May 20, 1968, ready once more to work hard.

4. Los Angeles
USC
Master of Arts
in Journalism

When we arrived in Los Angeles, we were greeted by a number of friends from Oregon. Mr. Yae and Mr. Min were very helpful in finding us a place to stay. The Rev. JH Park of Four Square Church, who was a leader of the Korean community, helped us find ways to survive in L.A. The church was located near the intersection of 8thStreet and Vermont. We rented the whole second floor of a house just behind the church. 2831-B 8th Street was our address. It was a very convenient location to commute to downtown Los Angeles and to shop in the area around Olympic Boulevard, which is now known as "Korea Town."

The University of Southern California 1970

Once we found a place to stay, we were desperate to find work to save money for the hospital costs for the arrival of a new member to our family. Young's pregnancy was becoming noticeable, but she managed to find work in a purse manufacturing factory. It was known as a "sweat shop," but she did not mind working under substandard conditions. The factory liked her so much that they let her continue working after a short maternity leave when Eugene was born.

With only a BA degree in journalism, I could not find a reasonable place to work in my profession. I went to the LA Times and the LA Herald Examiner and applied to work as a photographer. I was not sure I could report for these newspapers. I waited for some time and went to the Herald Examiner, which was surrounded by union members with placards reading "On Strike." I was hesitant to cross the picket line, but I was really desperate to do anything by that time.

When I went into the personnel office, an old lady who seemed to be responsible asked me to come into her office and explained the situation of the union strike at the paper to me. She said the paper could not afford to hire any professional staff, but the production department desperately needed workers like pressmen. She added that I should know about working conditions under a strike. I was so desperate that I signed the employment paper as a pressman with a note that I would be considered for a photographer position should any vacancy arise.

The union strike had started as the first case of the disputes that arose in adopting computer technology for the typesetting process of newspapers. It was an historic case that brought about the future collapse of the newspaper. A word processing computer program was not yet in existence, but the IBM 360 series was already being used by the banking industry punching computer cards and paper tapes.

The newspaper adopted a similar technique to set type by punching tapes, but many members of the typesetters' union were about to lose their jobs and decided to go on strike. Other unions like the teamsters who drove delivery trucks, joined the typesetters. There were fierce fights by the union with a number of shootings aimed at the "scabs."

I became a scab sometime early in June 1968 and even worked many overtime hours when I could do more than 40 hours a week. It was scary, but this produced sizable paychecks. I always volunteered to work on holidays and weekends so that I could save enough money for the upcoming child. Young and I were doing well finally, and we were even thinking about bringing over Susan and Anthony soon.

For my employment, I needed to file a petition to the U. S. Government for a work permit, but it was rejected on the grounds that my work was not in the category of professional. I was requested to report my departure date for Korea or to go to graduate school to maintain my student visa status. Actually, I had wanted to go to the University of Southern California for my Master's degree at some points. I went to USC and was admitted to the program that had already started.

Eugene's 1st Nirthday   August 7, 1969

Once again I had two jobs. I became a full time student, which was required by law, but I did not cut down my work hours with the Herald Examiner. On the 17th day of August, I was working, and I had made an arrangement with Mr. and Mrs. Min to take Young to the emergency room of any hospital close to our apartment. Her delivery time came and I wasn't there, the Mins took her to North Hollywood Presbyterian Hospital without knowing the hospital was a rather expensive one.

When I rushed to the hospital, Eugene was already born, a healthy eight pound and six ounce boy, which was not usual for an Asian baby. Fortunately both mother and newborn were doing fine. What a happy moment for us to have the child. My friend Min, however, was having trouble with his beetle VW that he had bought just a few days earlier. He was not an experienced driver. He drove into the wrong section of the hospital and then tried to back up the car against the gate protection device and ruined the two rear tires. I was more than happy to replace his tires, but I still tease him with what he did.

Los Angeles 1969

The hospital released Young and Eugene after two nights, and they moved to our apartment. Now, I realized, I had three jobs at the same time. Even though Young was healthy and eager to take care of the baby, I had to do a lot of things for both mother and child. The birth of Eugene, however, brought much good fortune, and we, as well as many of our friends in Los Angeles called him a lucky boy. Everything we intended became successful without a hitch since the birth of Eugene.

Before the end of 1968, our petitions to become permanent residents were approved. We were among the first group of beneficiaries of Lyndon B. Johnson's new immigration law of 1965. Until that law, it was not easy for aliens from Asia to become permanent residents who could be naturalized after five years. There were many Koreans who had come as students but did not finish their degrees, and stayed on as illegal aliens. They really admired what we had achieved.

After Eugene's birth, we bought another car, a 1965 Chevrolet Impala sedan, which had not been driven much by an old couple in the Hollywood area. The car was almost in mint condition, and we used it for many years until I became an assistant professor at the University of Missouri.

We drove the new car to Big Bear Mountains for the first time with friends. We were relaxed enough to drive around the country. Since Eugene had been born at an exclusive hospital, which released our information to land developing companies, we were invited to take a trip to Palm Springs which was being developed at that time. The company provided us with lavish meals and a bus trip to the area and encouraged us to buy one house lot for just $2,500. They also made a financial arrangement for us to pay the amount over many years and asked us to put only $250 down, which we did have, but we did not take the offer. We were interested in bringing our two older children over from Korea. I went back to Palm Springs many years later and found that I had missed the opportunity to be a neighbor of Bob Hope and his famous golf course!

Eugene grew up as a healthy child who drank more than half a gallon of milk every day. He woke up around three in the morning and asked for milk. Since Mom was going to work early in the morning, I was the one to take care of the baby at night. The young baby even liked me more than his baby sitter, Mrs. Kim, who always complained that I was the spoiler of Eugene.

My course work for my Master's degree went very smoothly, and I received the degree in January 1970 after only one and half years. Then I was able to enjoy more time with Eugene for a while until I had the next decision to make. If I stopped pursuing a degree after the completion of my Master's degree, we could have had a comfortable life as permanent residents and brought our two children from Korea to make a happy family. That was one possibility.

We used to go to New Peking, a Chinese restaurant owned and operated by Koreans. Mrs. Yae worked there as a cook, and we enjoyed a Chinese style noodle soup there. One day we met Sonia Seok, who was a well-known realtor among Koreans when the Korean population was less than 6,000. She encouraged me to pursue a career as a developer/realtor, which made good sense to me at that time. What would have happened if I had chosen a career as a realtor when the Korean population had just started to expand? I would be a very rich man, but I would not have reached my goal of getting a doctoral degree.

I decided to enroll in a doctoral program. USC unfortunately did not have a doctoral program in journalism at that time. The only school that had one on the west coast was Stanford, which admitted me without a scholarship. The University of Iowa, while not on the West Coast, offered a guarantee of an assistantship. So I decided to move to Iowa City in August to start the program. Young was hesitant about taking the risk but agreed with me to embark on the adventure. I am still grateful for her support of my plan all the way.

5. Iowa City
University of
Iowa
Ph.D. in Mass
Communication

We sent the necessary forms and money to bring Susan and Anthony to Iowa City. We already had our green cards, permanent resident visas that made our kids' trip quite simple. Susan was already in the second grade in a Daegu school, and Anthony was not in school yet in 1970. We were extremely excited about the prospect that our two loved ones would be coming.

Our friends in Los Angeles yelled at us when we told them we were going to Iowa. They did not seem to understand what we were trying to do. Many of them who had not achieved their academic goals told us that we would be coming back to Los Angeles after one or more years. Nevertheless, we had a great farewell party at the Korean Church, and they wished us the best for my academic pursuits.

On the way to Iowa City, stayed in Las Vegas August 1970

We packed everything we had into the 1965 Chevy Impala and left Los Angeles for Iowa City during the first week of August 1970. Eugene was not quite two years old but behaved like a grown-up child during our trip. We took the so-called southern route by taking interstate 40 and stopped over at a few tourists' spots on the way.

After a five hours drive, we arrived in Las Vegas. We stayed at the Sands Casino, where the Kim Sisters were performing, but we did not see the performance because of the high cost of tickets. Old Sands Casino was re-built by Steve Wynn and became the Wynn Casino now. I have been told that currently playing a round of golf at the Wynn costs you $500. Money doesn't seem to mean much in Las Vegas.

We left early in the morning the next day and stopped over at the Grand Canyon. Then we continued to drive to Flagstaff, where we found a Chinese restaurant and checked in a motel. While climbing the Rocky Mountains, we were shocked to come across a snow storm in August. Everything we saw on the road was new to us, and we stopped over many tourist spots in Arizona and New Mexico.

Hawkeye Campus, Iowa City

We were not in a hurry. We stopped over in Amarillo, Texas, to check the tires and other things in the heavily loaded car. We also had to re-fill the ice box for Eugene's milk and our food. We drove to the state of Missouri and took Highway 65 to go north to Interstate 80 that led directly to Iowa City.

When we arrived in Iowa City, we checked in to the assigned married student housing unit in the Finkbine area. Many barracks were built after WWII to accommodate a large number of returning students. The area looked like a military camp, and the University already was planning to demolish the barracks to make a parking lot for the medical school. A round metal barrack was divided into two units, and each unit had two bedrooms, a kitchen and a living room.

When we moved in to the barracks in August, Iowa's weather was not so hot. As winter approached, we had an oil burning stove to heat the unit just like what we saw in war movies. We had no complaints as two other Korean students lived there for a while, and we were told we would be relocated next year to the modern type of apartment in the Hawkeye Drive area.

Susan and Anthony arrived in Iowa City   December 1970

We had savings of $3,000, but we had to spend quite a bit of the money to furnish the unit. A refrigerator was the most expensive item, and we bought basic furniture from garage sales. We had to prepare for the arrival of our two older children.

I was an experienced student after receiving two degrees and knew what I had to do for the completion of my final degree. I signed up for more than 17 credit hours a semester and planned well ahead to complete my requirements in two years. I also asked Dr. Mal MacLean, the director of the school for help with my plan to complete my requirements faster than other students. Dr. MacLean was a strong supporter, who understood my sense of urgency as a father of three children.

As a doctoral student, I was supported with one half-time assistantship that paid $480 a month. We were supposed to work 20 hours a week for a professor, but my professor Bill Zima never asked me to do much for either his research or his teaching. Instead I used his office as mine when he was not in it, especially at night.

Happy Susan, Eugene and Anthony on Christmas Day in Toronto Canada

As we were expecting to support a five-member family, my assistantship alone was not enough. Young asked Mrs. Lim, who was working in a tooth-brush company in town, to help her find work. She started her swing shift from four in the afternoon until midnight. It was hard work, but I never heard her complain.

Eugene was only a few weeks older than two, when I had to start taking care of him everyday after four in the afternoon. While I worked in the apartment, I had been having Eugene watch some children's comic programs on television. When I had some errands to run, I usually found a TV program and had Eugene sit on the couch to watch the show while I was gone, Eugene never had any problem.

One day that September, I had gone to the university computer center to run one of the lengthy programs. In 1970, we used punched computer cards for programming, feeding them into the reader and waiing for a while to get our output printouts. When we found mistakes, we had to correct them on the cards and feed them again. I was caught up running the program and did not go back to Eugene for about three or four hours.

Eugene apparently had been crying aloud when he saw scary scenes. One of our neighbor students, who had never been friendly to anybody, called the police, and the police called the County's Family Services. They told me they would take Eugene with them if I did not know how to take care of a small child. I explained what had happened, and they left after giving me a warning that such a case should not happen again. I was scared to death and never left him alone again.

In the middle of my first semester, around the first week of October, we were informed that Susan and Anthony were coming to Chicago's O'Hare Airport. Travel arrangements for two children who knew not a word of English were made by my brother Won-heung and his wife. Susan, seven years old and Anthony, five years old had huge name tags, on which our address, phone number and their travel plan were printed. When Won-heung and his wife went to the Kimpo airport, they found a couple who were going to Philadelphia and asked them to take care of the children on their way to the Chicago airport.

When the plane arrived in Chicago, the couple escorted our children to the exit gates. The KAL staff in Chicago helped them go through the Customs and Immigration. After four years, we finally had our whole family together. Two year-old Eugene knew what was happening and welcomed his big sister and elder brother. It was late in the night when we drove to Iowa City, but we continued telling our endless stories.

As a second grader Susan remembered us well and called us Mom and Dad when we hugged her at the airport. However, Anthony seemed to be puzzled by the many drastic changes and could not call us Mom and Dad right away. He had been about one year old when I left. But both children seem to be very happy to be with their parents in America. And we did everything they wanted in order to pay them back for what we owed to them for the last four years apart. I even went out to buy new bicycles for Susan and Anthony.

After a few days of rest, both children went to the local school, where Susan was in the second grade and Anthony in the kindergarten. They did not know one English word, but they were catching up fast, and they did not have any problem at school. I checked with the teachers, who surprisingly told me that they were doing just fine, and that they might speak better English than mine soon.

I was very busy with my school work, driving Young to work and babysitting after four in the afternoon. But we were very happy when the weekend or holidays came. We went fishing by the Coralville River and caught many big carp, Since we did not know how to cook them, we let them go.

We invited Young's sister and her family to Iowa City for Christmas. The family lived in Toronto, Canada, and had three children, Helen, Cecilia and Joseph. When they arrived at our apartment, they could not believe what they saw. They thought all Americans were doing well and expected to find a dream house like the one they had seen on television. Now all the three children are married and have their own families, but they vividly remember what they had seen in 1970. They really were terrible accommodations worse than some of the refugee camps during the war time. However, we were just happy to have our family together.

Susan started riding her bike and taught Anthony and other neighborhood children to ride her bike. She became a bossy figure in the neighborhood after they all came back from school. I asked her, how she found the rest room or communicated with other kids. It was not difficult at all, she said. She must have used sign language in the early days in Iowa City.

I had completed most of the required courses after three regular semesters and one summer session and had started on my dissertation early during my course work. I used to stay in Professor Zima's office during most of the nights. Another doctoral student John Lent also worked in the nights at Professor Markham's office. John, who had started his graduate work three years earlier than I had and finished his dissertation about the same time, had been good friends with the janitors, who came to clean the building. They often brought cookies and donuts for us and went out to get cigarettes when we asked them.

During the middle of the fourth semester, I was ready to defend my dissertation. On the 17th day of March, I passed the oral defense of my dissertation, which was the last item for my degree. Few faculty members or students knew what I had done. I completed my doctoral degree in one year and seven months, a record, I was not sure anybody else could beat. On my transcript, I had an A in all my courses except for one B.

Two other Korean students had started their programs one or more years ahead of me. They were shocked. I was using ATS (Administrative Terminal System), an earlier version of word processing, writing my dissertation. My doctoral committee members as well as other students did not know that system. The early version of word processing used a typewriter-like keyboard set without a monitor for the text input that was processed in the main computer, IBM 370 series. I had to wait for a while to get a printout to make corrections.

I did not hire a professional typist. I also used RJE (Remote Job Entry) system with telephone wire and coupler to make the connection between my workstation and the main computer. I was far ahead of everybody in the journalism school at that time. Now everybody uses word processing that makes it so easy to type letters and documents. I also produced a number of inquiry letters for my job application with the system. I could easily write a hundred letters in a matter of a few minutes. This knowledge really made a difference.

After the completion of the dissertation, I had accomplished what I had intended to do, and I should have gone back to Korea as promised. However, Susan, Anthony and Eugene were doing extremely well in school, so Young and I decided I would find a job in the States first. I was not getting any responding letters of interest and was frustrated. I wrote to SK Lee, a classmate of Korea University who was the secretary to the president of Korea University. He encouraged me to try in the States and suggested that coming back to Korea should be the last choice.

The commencement was on May 10, when I received the degree. I asked for University permission to stay in the University housing until the end of summer session. We were in a serious dilemma. I would have much better opportunities for my career if I went back to Korea as one of the earlier journalism degree holders. But we knew our children would have better education in the States.

During the last week of June, Dr. MacLean called me to come to his office. When I went into his office, he was all smiles and he told me that I might get a job that would be the best one for me. Dr. William Stephenson of the University of Missouri had requested that he send one of his graduating students to be a possible replacement for his position as he was thinking about retirement. He requested that the candidate should have the knowledge and skill of working with computers, and Dr. MacLean had responded, "We have a wonderful candidate." He told me I should go down to Columbia, Missouri, the following Monday as he had already made the arrangement.

It took about five hours to drive to Columbia, but I went there Sunday night, stayed in a motel and went to the Missouri School of Journalism early in the morning. Dr. Stephenson was waiting for me, and we discussed various subjects for a while.

The search committee, chaired by Milt Gross, Associate Dean of the school, was going to meet me in Flaming Pits restaurant at noon, and I went there to meet the members of the committee. They chatted about the school and asked me just a few questions. After the meeting, Milt smilingly told me, "the position is yours, but Dean Fisher is out of town. He will tell you the details of salary and contract when you meet him at the AEJ Convention in Carbondale."

After the lunch meeting, I called Young and told her we would be moving down to Missouri. I also visited some Korean professors on campus at that time, Soon Sung Cho, Keum Hee Lee and Heun Yong Kim. Dr. Cho was delighted to have a Korean professor in the journalism school. The school was established in 1908 as the first journalism school in the world and had hired no foreign professor since its establishment.

As I was told by Dr. MacLean, the Missouri journalism school was known as a professional education oriented school, which required a prior successful two-year media experience. I was not sure I met that requirement. But Dr. Stephenson liked me, and that was all that mattered. I met Dean Fisher at the convention, and he was very kind to explain my employment. Roy Fisher was a longtime Chicago journalist and managing editor of the Chicago Sun Times.

When I went back to Iowa City, Dr. MacLean and many others congratulated me, but they were very hesitant to talk about Missouri. I had a feeling that they wondered how long I could last in that highly professional setting. I was extremely happy to find a job at a school that was rated number one for journalism education in the world.

I drove down to Columbia one more time to find a house or apartment. Dr. Cho owned a second house on Clayton Street, and we decided to stay there for at least a year. I flew to Cedar Rapids after leaving the car in Missouri. We rented a fourteen foot long truck, packed everything we had and drove the truck to our next town, Columbia, where we stayed for more than 30 years.

Part III
My Career

1. Professor of Journalism University of Missouri

University of Missouri

Assistant Professor of Journalism

As a brand new Ph.D. and an assistant professor of journalism in the Missouri School of Journalism, I started my teaching career in the first and the most famous journalism school in the world. Everyone in journalism admired my job. However, the job was not so admirable to me at all.

As soon as I started my work, I sensed that I was in an alien world, where most of the administrators, staff members and faculty tried to show their kindness to the first alien member of the faculty, but I felt like they could not hide their feelings that I was one of those academicians with doctoral degrees who would not last long. The majority of faculties at school of journalism at that time had neither a doctoral degree, nor academic backgrounds. Roy Fisher, dean of the school who was appointed one year ahead of me, was a perfect example. He was a Chicago-based newspaperman, who had been a managing editor of the Chicago Sun Times.

One of the major tasks of the school was to run three media operations: a commercial newspaper, *The Columbia Missourian*; Channel 8, an NBC affiliated local television station; and KBIA, an NPR radio station, all of which were mostly staffed by students, who were getting real-world professional education and training.

The faculty who had extensive professional experience worked as the skeleton staff of the news operations. There, of course, were notable exceptions--Dr. William Stephenson, a distinguished advertising research professor, Donald Brenner and Keith P. Sanders, who both worked in a separate world of the graduate program.

I was assigned to the advertising department, which did not have much to do with the news operation, except that a few faculty members worked in the advertising section of the newspaper. I did not have any notable media experience and came out of the heavily academic Iowa program, which was not respected much at all after losing its accreditation. Missouri was in charge of accreditation at that time.

I was assigned to work in the graduate program, which was getting bigger and more popular. I was given a choice of two courses among six courses in theory and research methods. I was very fortunate to have a senior faculty member, Keith P. Sanders, who was also a graduate of Iowa and responsible for these courses. He helped me a great deal to survive in that situation.

It was a harsh reality for me that I needed to survive one more time facing insurmountable tasks of teaching and research. As a first-year appointee, I was not given any administrative work or student advising. I chose to teach "Theories of Mass Communication" and "Research Methods in Journalism," and I also needed to prepare to teach four other courses: Theories of Communication, Advanced Research Methods, Information Theories and Journalism as Communication.

It took a lot more effort to prepare to teach two courses than to take two classes as a student. A theory course was easier for me to prepare since the course was a required one for doctoral students and there were only 12 students in my first semester. But the research method course was packed with about 20 students, including some who took journalism because they hated math and statistics.

Most of the students had had experience working for the mass media and had decided to enroll in the graduate program at the University of Missouri. It was very difficult to motivate these journalists to learn statistics to make sense of social trends or to understand the complexities of quantitative data.

The only topic that interested those students was how to conduct election polls and how to write news stories with election poll statistics. I volunteered to be an advisor for the *Columbia Missourian* for the election poll coverage and required my students to conduct a telephone survey during elections as a part of the course assignments. I spent time in the newsroom and got acquainted with faculty members working for the paper. As I taught my graduate students how to conduct election polls and write stories with the data for the Missourian, I played an important role for the paper as a faculty supervisor for election polls and survey data of social trends. I did my share of working for a commercial newspaper and gained valuable practical experience.

I also brought in the SPSS (Statistical Package for Social Science) software for the students to analyze survey data. The software had been widely used in the University of Iowa program, but the Missouri journalism school had not yet begun to use this simple package. Students were amazed how the old IBM 370 series could read the computer cards punched with IBM 029 machines and turn out massive analyses of data. The back alley of the old graduate center in the Walter Williams Hall became a computer center of the school, and I could hire graduate assistants for data processing.

At the end of the first semester, I received a barely passing grade in evaluations done by the students and the department chair and saw a glimpse of my future in teaching in the school. At the same time I had worked hard to bring in new developments in computer programs such as ATS (Administrative Terminal System), which was the starting point of IBM's word processing software, and some remote entry operations with IBM equipment.

My work was noted by the campus computing operations, and I was invited to develop word processing software. It was 1972; I was on top of the pioneering stage of computers when Bill Gates was still in high school.

What helped me a lot to build my popularity among staff members was the humble attitude, I had maintained from the beginning. When I first met one of the senior staff members, she called me "Dr. Chang," but I sincerely asked her to call me "Won," since I was not going to treat any patient and wasn't paid as much. She thought it was funny at first but became my strong supporter later. A couple of years later, another Iowa graduate, who had some media experience, was hired, but the young American had an opposite attitude. He asked the staff member "call me Dr. so and so," when she called him Bob. He did not stay with us after his first year.

I worked hard on my research and publications to survive and was recognized as a strong researcher when I published a number of articles in the *Journalism Quarterly*, the most recognized publication in the field. I published more than what was required in refereed journals during my first five years. My publication record helped me to be appointed as a doctoral faculty by the campus community, and I was promoted to Associate Professor one year ahead of the usual schedule.

I worked hard at my teaching and learned to deal with a large class of under-graduate students. I created a new course in advertising research and several interna-tional advertising courses that I enjoyed teaching. Teaching large undergraduate courses was the final step required to be promoted to a full professor. I made it in ten years.

I was asked by the dean to coach a distinguished journalist in 1975, the sci-ence editor of the Associated Press, who had been invited to teach a semester as a part of the Professional in Residence program. The career journalist was told by the dean and other faculty members that teaching should be easy for him as he just needed to tell the students anecdotes of what and how he covered science stories for AP for thirty some years. Right after the first class, he came to me with a surprised face of excitement and told me that he had told all of his stories during the first class, and that he was feeling anxious, about how he could cover the next 16 weeks of the semester. I worked with him to stretch his materials over 16 weeks and coached him on what to do.

Another untold part of a faculty qualification was to be an accepted col-league among the faculty with a reputable social character and an agreeable attitude. I was told in the early stage of my career in Missouri that I might have some prob-lems in this area, since I came from another culture. However, I was very careful not to be out of bounds, such as getting a reputation for drinking. I never had more than two drinks during any type of party with faculty members. I also actively participat-ed in many types of faculty social gatherings. It wasn't hard; it was my nature any-way.

Advanced Probability Seminar (APS), a poker club, existed way before I arrived. Members met every other Thursdays in a host house and played poker from seven to midnight. The rotating host needed to prepare beer and snacks. Some folks prepared more elaborate dishes, and our home became known to have delicious egg rolls made by Young with a variety of vegetables. It was a nickel and dime game, but some members needed more than twenty dollars just to stay in the games. I, an inscrutable Oriental, was known as a winner who played well in the games.

I also joined the Journalism School's golf and bowling teams that competed with members of other departments. I won many prizes for playing golf, but I did not do well bowling with an average of 160 pins after trying more than 25 years. Playing these sports provided me ample opportunities to meet campus administra-tors and faculty leaders. I was also very active on campus committees, representing the Journalism School in the faculty promotion and tenure committee.

I worked with doctoral students and supervised 31 dissertations, which was a record in our program when I retired in 2000. I actually told other faculty members that my philosophy of teaching doctoral students was to work with them, not be a supervisor. I actively participated in students' research and motivated them to complete their dissertations. I used to call some of my doctoral students early in the morning to share my suggestions for their research. One doctoral student's wife came up with a response for my call, saying "he is taking a shower now, and he will call you soon." She did not wake up her husband, who had stayed up late into the night.

As I settled down with tenure in the school, there were a few niches; I could develop such as international programs by bringing in journalists from Asia and other parts of the world. John C. Merrill, a well-known journalism educator, who was a pioneer in the international journalism program. He was interested in bringing in Latin American journalists to the Missouri graduate program. In 1973, he was brave enough to propose a Plan C that replaced the requirements of courses in reporting and editing for the school media with theory courses.

We already had Plan A that required writing a Master's thesis and Plan B that required working in Washington, D.C., Jefferson City and London reporting programs. Most of the journalists from outside the States had major difficulties in passing the media courses because of the language barrier. Since they would go back to their countries to continue practicing journalism, according to Merrill, they just needed to take more theory courses to make up for the media requirement. The faculty reluctantly approved the program, which lasted more than 20 years.

Within a few years of the operation of Plan C, John Merrill, creator and director, moved on to be the director of Louisiana State University, and I was appointed the director of our program until the program was absorbed into the Missouri graduate program in 1986. The program served international students from all over the world well. There were a few Korean students early in the graduate program, but the benefit of Plan C really went to Korean students who were recruited after my first trip back to Korea in 1975.

As the Director of the Plan C program, I also was the advisor to Taiwanese students, who would not get along well with the Snow fellows. One of the Taiwanese students at that time was a colonel, who was sent by the Taiwanese military. I had many tense situations that I had to handle fairly for both groups. But all of the Chinese students were great people, who completed their studies and became leaders of academic and media operations back in China.

The benefits of wearing these two hats for me included a number of trips to Taiwan and Beijing. I made almost annual visits to these places as a distinguished guest and was treated well. In Beijing, Feng Xiliang of Beijing Review, a Missouri journalism graduate in 1949, was to establish an English newspaper, The China Daily in 1981. We helped him publish the first English newspaper in Beijing since 1949 Feng became the managing editor of the paper and sent a number of his staff members to our school. He later worked as the editor-in-chief until his retirement. Feng also received the Missouri Journalism Honor Medal in 1984. Feng invited me in 1991 to be a guest speaker for the 10th anniversary of the paper, where I suggested that the paper raise its advertising fees to help make it a money-making medium.

Director of the Edgar Snow Program

After 1979 when President Nixon made a surprise visit to China, our school was invited to train Chinese journalists. Dean Fisher made a trip to China and established the Edgar Snow Program, which would bring in about 12 Chinese professionals to our program to complete their Master's degree in two years. Our school provided financial support for those students, who would become the leaders of Chinese journalism. The dean was really excited about the program and appointed me as the Director.

The first nine journalists in 1980, three from Radio Beijing, three from Xinhua News Agency and three from Beijing Review were the brightest top-notch journalists selected from the huge number of applicants. There were three outstanding fellows: Wu Xiaoyong of Radio Beijing, Liu Quizong of Xinhua and Liu Yoan of Beijing Review, who became leaders of the Chinese media. Wu was the son of Wu Xueqian, the Chinese minister of foreign affairs at that time.

It was 1980, and the FBI had been closely watching these Chinese journalists. I was visited by an agent in Jefferson City at least once a month and was asked to tell the agent anything important. I repeatedly told him nothing important had happened. Then one day in November, Simon, a Snow fellow, was arrested by the local police for shoplifting in a drugstore. He was accused of hiding a pair of woman's stockings in his pocket. Dean Fisher was called by the Chinese embassy in Washington and went to the police station. Simon was released without any record. But this incident did not go away without severe punishment by the Chinese authorities. Simon did stay in the program, but did not go back to Beijing.

The first nine journalists in 1980, three from Radio Beijing, three from Xinhua News Agency and three from Beijing Review were the brightest top-notch journalists selected from the huge number of applicants. There were three outstanding fellows: Wu Xiaoyong of Radio Beijing, Liu Quizong of Xinhua and Liu Yoan of Beijing Review, who became leaders of the Chinese media. Wu was the son of Wu Xueqian, the Chinese minister of foreign affairs at that time.

It was 1980, and the FBI had been closely watching these Chinese journalists. I was visited by an agent in Jefferson City at least once a month and was asked to tell the agent anything important. I repeatedly told him nothing important had happened. Then one day in November, Simon, a Snow fellow, was arrested by the local police for shoplifting in a drugstore. He was accused of hiding a pair of woman's stockings in his pocket. Dean Fisher was called by the Chinese embassy in Washington and went to the police station. Simon was released without any record. But this incident did not go away without severe punishment by the Chinese authorities. Simon did stay in the program, but did not go back to Beijing.

My first trip to China was in 1984, but it was a brief visit. In 1986, I visited China for four weeks, during which I had opportunities to meet senior officials of the Chinese media, I went to the Fudan University in Shanghai and gave a series of lectures to journalism students. I also visited the Yanbian Korean region in Manchuria and climbed to the top of the Baikdu Mountain. My report of the trip was published extensively in the Joongang Daily for its anniversary issue.

In Taipei, Ma Shingya, chairman of the Board of the Central News Agency and a Missouri graduate of 1942, also received his honor medal on my recommendation at the same time with Feng. Ma, a staff member of Generalissimo Chiang and the senior head of the Taiwanese media, invited me as a national guest to Taipei, and I was honored to give a .speech. The audience included military generals, deans of journalism schools and leaders of the media. It was all very exciting and challenging.

Sabbatical leave

I had taken my sabbatical leave in 1980, and gone to Korea University for a semester. I went alone since all my children were in schools, and Young had full-time work with the Shelter Insurance Company. I was also appointed as a visiting professor at Sophia University in Tokyo, Japan, where I spent a few months during the semester. It was not difficult to manage to travel to Tokyo. Fortunately, I had a faculty apartment in the center of the most expensive city in the world at that time, because Korea University was in turmoil with student protests against the military rule of the country.

The military general who was elected as the President, Chun Du-hwan, was interested in recruiting university professors into politics and one of my close friends became a top member of his government. He asked me to join him in politics. Without hesitation, I refused and went back to Missouri. I have often wondered if I had joined with Chun, what would have been the outcome of my life. I think I would have died of a heart attack, been sent to prison, or made a fortune and became rich and famous. I do not regret what I did that time.

As a Fulbright Scholar in 1987

Fulbright Senior Professor to Korea University in 1987

A Fulbright senior faculty fellowship was hard to get, but it came with many benefits and much recognition. I was getting my salary from Missouri while I was paid well by Korea University, the host institution, and Fulbright Commission. I also received a pass to enter the U.S. embassy in Seoul and was treated as a member of the diplomatic corps of the U.S. government. I could use the embassy commissary, where I could shop for exotic items like fine Scotch whiskies, groceries and fruit without tax. I could also visit military installations where good restaurants served inexpensive foods. Young and I used these restaurants a lot to entertain our friends who, indeed, enjoyed the unusual opportunities.

`   I also bought a used car that I drove all over the country to see people and places where I wanted to visit whenever I had the opportunity. One of the most memorable trips was to the Sorak Mountain in the fall. The rocky mountain was so colorful. We were provided with the best suite of the Sorak Tourist Hotel by a friend who was the chief of Sokcho County. Other areas of our travel were famous Buddhist temples where we enjoyed watching their meditation and eating vegetarian foods.

Being a Fulbright fellow, I was invited to give speeches to US information offices in provincial capitals. I went down to Kwangju when emotions in the town were rather tense after the Korean military had overpowered the citizens' militant protests in 1980. Residents blamed the Americans who did not stop the military action, but I was talking about new information technologies that would affect Korean media and society. I was treated well there. I also went down to Busan for a similar arrangement.

I had to teach two courses in the host institution, Korea University, but I also was requested to teach courses at Ewha Women's University, Kyunghee University and Hankook University of Foreign Studies.

Associate Dean for Graduate Studies and Research

One other area I explored was being an administrator. In 1991, Ed Lambeth resigned from his position of Associate Dean for Graduate Studies and Research, and Dean Mills asked me to take over on an interim basis until we found a permanent replacement. The job consisted of massive workload with about 40 graduate faculty members, and 220 Master students and 20 doctoral students. I was very hesitant, but I took the challenge. I delegated most of the routine paperwork to a very experienced academic advisor who seemed to know every detail of our graduate program and managed well without having any student protest or submit agrievance.

The biggest challenge for me was to chair monthly graduate faculty meetings. Each of the 40 faculty members seemed to have an independent opinion about our graduate program, and any change in the program would be very difficult to initiate at the faculty meetings. The chair of the meeting needed very skillful maneuvers to bring about consensus after various views were presented. I handled most of the agenda items pretty well, but some issues could not be resolved at the meeting. In those cases, I would form a subcommittee to review the issue and report back to the next meeting. Most of the tabled items were not resolved during my tenure of 18 months.

Chancellor Kiesler and Deans' Visit to Chosun Ilbo 1994

Chancellor Kisler to Korea in 1993

Around November 1992, Dr. Charles Kiesler was hired to be the Chancellor of the University. The new head of our University started his aggressive and ambitious plan to make MU a top notch University. He hired Brady Deaton, a professor of international agricultural economics, as the chief of staff, a position previously not known to this 200-year-old campus, which operated like the White House. One of Kiesler's plans was to increase the size of the endowment fund, which was not comparable with other highly prestigious private universities.

It did not take long for Kiesler to find a "niche point of Korea," which was exactly what he said in the planning committee as he began to organize a well-planned trip to Korea. The Chancellor's Trip to Korea Committee was formed with one representative from each of 14 academic divisions. I, as the representative of the school of journalism, was the key person for the committee, which decided the participating members of the trip. Under the new leadership of Kiesler, every dean wanted to go, but only four deans would be selected; journalism, agriculture, the business school and arts and science, along with the campus development head, Jane Irvine and John Hyle, director of the international program.

The objectives of the trip were spelled out. The first on the list was to get a $450,000 endowment fund from the International Exchange Fund of the Korea Foundation, which was originally approved but canceled after a year. The new chairman of the Korea Foundation was a brother-in-law of the newly elected President Y.S. Kim and a good friend of mine, who had graduated from the same department of political science of the same university a year later and who would not say "no" to what I asked for. Everything was worked out in detail to get the fund, and the Chancellor was to show up for the signing ceremony of the endowment.

The second objective was to get an endowment from a leading newspaper in Korea, the Chosun Ilbo, which was awarded the distinguished Missouri Journalism Award in 1986. I was informed that the top newspaper was willing to establish an endowment. There were other possibilities from agriculture and economics colleges, which produced a large number of Korean Ph. D.s, who were taking main positions in the government offices in their fields. The chancellor was also scheduled to visit the Sungkok Journalism Foundation, which supported the Columbia Missourian building with $250,000.

The trip plan was worked out in detail, but I found out that the Chancellor, his wife and Dean Mills were booked in the economy class according to a requirement of state law while I was booked in the business class. MU was a state institu-

tion, which was supported with state funding, and only the governor could fly in business class while all the others were supposed to fly in economy class. During all my years at MU, I never paid the business fare but managed to fly in business class most of the time. With the help of CW KIM of the Joongang Daily Newspaper, I helped make arrangements for more comfortable seating on the second deck of the 747 for the 14-hour flight from Chicago. I also managed to fly them back to Chicago in business class. The Kieslers never thanked me enough for the arrangements I'd made.

We had a tight schedule. We arrived in the afternoon of Friday and had a luncheon in the Phoenix Room of the Hilton Hotel, hosted by JW Hahn, President of the Sungkok Journalism Foundation. The Korea Herald reported our trip the following day in great detail written by a reporter, who had studied in Missouri. Sunday was spent on a tour of the palaces in Seoul with my son Anthony volunteering to be the tour guide.

The schedule was really heavy the following Monday. We went to the Korea Foundation for the signing ceremony of the $1,1 million endowment and received the first year's allotment of $100,000. It was a very gratifying ceremony for us. Our luncheon was hosted by the *DongA Ilbo* at the Lotte Hotel, and we met the Minister of Education followed by a meeting with the Prime Minister, Young-deuk Lee, in the afternoon.

I also prepared to give plaques of Distinguished Achievement in Journalism to Yongsoon Shin (deceased), Younghee Kim, Jino Ha (deceased), Jongil Eun, Dukkyu Kim, Yongseung Lee, Janghan Rhee, Inhyung Lee (deceased),

Missouri Chancellor Kiesler,s Visit to Korea 1994

Joohyun Lee, Sangwon Lim, Yongsang Park, Byungkoo Hahn (deceased) and Kwangjae Lee at the ceremony in the press room of the Seoul Press Center later that day.

After the ceremony we all were invited to a special reception in the Heuk-suk-dong residence of Sanghoon Bahng, publisher of the Chosun Ilbo, where we were bombarded with drinks.

We also had meetings with the Presidents of Korea University and Hanyang University, where we signed exchange agreements for our contribution to scholarships and support for Korean students. We also visited the Office of Agricultural Development in Suwon, which our university had been supporting to developing agricultural technologies since the Korean War.

It was a busy one week working trip, which produced substantial outcomes, and the Chancellor was extremely pleased with the way our schedule worked out. But some other members were not as happy about the "super punctual" way I had arranged our schedule. I received a nickname, "super punctual" after the trip. After the trip, the Chancellor invited me and my wife to his box to watch a football game. We were escorted by the campus police to the elevator, checked in the Chancellor's box, which was air-conditioned. We were served refreshment, watched the game and were escorted again home. It was a great experience.

There was a rumor that I might be appointed a vice chancellor, but Kiesler was fired by the Board of Curators the next year. I not only lost my chance to be working for the campus administration, but I became identified as a "Kiesler man" who was not popular after the changeover.

Advertising Faculty Members 1992

Advertising Department Chairman

I was elected by the faculty in 1995 to be the advertising department chair for three years. We had the largest student enrollment while the number of faculty in the department was only ten. When I took over the chairmanship, we had two unhappy faculty members who repeatedly threatened the dean and the chair with legal suits. The salaries of faculty members were adjusted based on the evaluations of their teaching, research and service to the school. The final evaluation was done by the committee consisting of department chairs and deans, but the letter informing the faculty member of the outcome of evaluations was written by the department chair. The job of writing those evaluation letters was the hardest thing I experienced. I sure didn't regret giving that up.

2. Ajou University
Suwon, Korea

Ajou University in Suwon Korea

Teaching in Korea has been one of my career goals. The main reason why I came to the United States for my education and degrees was to get a teaching career in Korea. I had repeatedly tried to settle in Korea but never had the opportunity to do so. My first attempt was in 1980 when I took a six months leave and taught at Korea University.

Ajou students after lecture 2000

But Korean society was in turmoil at that time after the assassination of President Park, and our children, who were in high school would not consider moving to Korean schools. Then I was awarded a senior Fulbright Fellowship to Korea University in 1987 when I was doing my most productive work at the University of Missouri and decided to stay in the States.

Ten years later, as my retirement was coming closer, I had the chance to think about it one more time. In 1997 when I reached my 60th birthday, I asked for a sabbatical leave for one year from Missouri and decided to teach as a Distinguished Professor of Information and Communication at Ajou University in Suwon Korea. Dr. Duk Joong Kim, president of the university, persuaded me to do so, and he insisted that I should stay there until my retirement. I wanted to see how this arrangement would work. President Kim gave my wife and me his own apartment on campus, and my teaching appointment was also worked out.

Ajou University did not have a journalism or communication department, and I was assigned to the College of Information and Communication, which was a computer science school with a heavy emphasis on information and telecommunication technology. I created two courses: one in advertising principles and practice, and the other in communication theories to help students learn a wider perspective in dealing with target groups of clients. I also was asked to teach these courses in English, which made my teaching easier, but I had more difficulties motivating students to read English textbooks and other reading materials. They really struggled to follow my instructions in English.

After two semesters in Korea, I was getting used to the Korean system of higher education and enjoyed teaching Korean students and relationships with Korean faculty members. But I was forced to go back to Missouri for at least one year as part of the sabbatical requirement. I promised Ajou University that I would come back after my retirement.

When I came back to Missouri in August 1998 and resumed my teaching, I was prepared to take my retirement after at least three years, which would put my service to the university at more than 30 years, qualifying me for a fairly good benefit package. I also decided to retire in Missouri, where I could have the best medical care and enjoy my relationships with many friends and retirees of the university. I started to renovate the Highridge house with a new wooden patio and front garden.

Around the end of the first semester, it was announced that the Ufrniversity was going to offer an early retirement package that simply added three more years of service to the retirement calculation. It was perfect timing and a golden opportunity for me. I did not hesitate to take the offer, which actually gave me 33 years service with my summer teachings included. Other journalism faculty members including my good friend Keith Sanders also took the offer. I immediately notified Dr. Kim that I might be able to join Ajou in 2000. At Ajou University I was appointed a regular member of the faculty, who could receive all the benefits which visiting faculty members would not receive.

Three More Years (2000-2003): Since I had decided to retire in Columbia, Missouri, I had to rent the house out for three years until I reached the mandatory retirement age of 65. Young-Ja, my youngest sister and her two sons moved in so that the boys could attend Hickman High School. We would use her house in Bang-bae-dong, Seoul, for a year. After two years of their stay, Dr. TC Jung of Busan, who was taking his sabbatical year, was given the house to stay in for a year without paying rent. Everything seemed to fit perfectly, and I started my two-year plan of teaching at Ajou University again.

The first thing I wanted to try was to offer a large "Mass Media and Society" class that would be open to all to attract students from various disciplines and would be taught in Korean. It was a great idea, which attracted more than 100 students from many disciplines including nursing. I managed it for one semester, but it took way too much of my time and effort preparing for lectures and grading exams without teaching assistants. I struggled hard without getting the expected results. The worst part of the experiment was my lecture room, which was like a flat warehouse without air-conditioning and audio equipment. I had to give up my dream of becoming a super professor in Korea and found another role as a faculty advisor to the campus newspaper.

Ajou University Newspaper: During the early days of my first semester, I was invited to have a lunch with President Kim, who asked me to take over the faculty advisor position of the University Press, a campus radio station and an English-language student magazine. It was a total surprise for me, and I tried to decline the offer, since I knew well how difficult it was to deal with student press not only in the States but also in Korea. But I could not reject the President's firm request and took over the chore that I had successfully avoided during my career in the States.

Ajou Newspaper   Student reporters 2000

During my stay in Ajou for the next three years, which included a one-year extension to the original two-year contract, I was devoted to working with the students of the campus newspaper. I found it the most rewarding experience while teaching classes had become a routine, similar to what I had done in Missouri. I wanted to be an excellent lecturer, but my English instruction and lectures were mismatches with Ajou students. But teaching in English made my life easier, and I could spend more time with student reporters and editors, whom I charmed like a grandfather.

Ajou University Press, a biweekly campus paper, had a long tradition of independent editorial policy, which had not tolerated any faculty or university censorship for thirty some years. C.K. Park, editor of the paper in August 2000, and nine reporters were alarmed that an American professor who was older than their parents would become their advisor, but they were quickly relieved when they met me for the first time. I told them I would do exactly what an American professor would do for the campus newspaper. I would not ask what the top story would be, or any details of controversial issues of the University.

I would be available for advice until publication. However, I would be very harsh in dealing with their mistakes if I found any.

One of the major contributions I could make for the University was to open the door for students to global perspectives. Korean students, I felt, needed to see what was going on outside the peninsula. I persuaded President Kim to allow us go on a reporting trip in January the following year to the United States, where we would visit the University of Missouri to explore journalism issues, the University of Florida for language instructions for se-lected Ajou freshmen, and Stanford University for campus life. This was the first time in the history of the University that students had such an opportuni-ty to travel abroad for reporting.

The Ajou students and I had gotten along really well as we worked together for the publication of the campus paper. I also suggested a number of ideas for reporting campus issues, such as student polls as I had done for the Columbia Missourian. Students did a wonderful job in publishing papers on time despite some mistakes that nobody seemed to notice. After the publi-cation of each issue, I critiqued it, and then we all moved to a nearby restau-rant, where we continued our discussion on reporting. Our favorite restaurant was managed by a couple who knew what we liked--a simple bacon slab not

Ajou Reporting Team at the University of Missouri
2001

smoked or seasoned, which we called "three layer pork meats." The young people had big appetites and consumed a lot of meat and soju. After the meal, we would move to a draft beer joint to celebrate more of our recent publications. Sometimes we also moved on to a Karaoke bar. But I was generations apart from these young people.

Ajou students also had an opportunity to see how a doctoral committee would work. H.S. Kim, a doctoral student under my supervision, completed his dissertation while I was in Suwon. I arranged to have his final defense committee meeting during our stay in Columbia. Kim already had his Master's degree in broadcasting and worked as a newscaster for the Korean Broadcasting System. He was an excellent presenter in English. His presentation with PowerPoint was superb in many respects as he explained the highlights of his research for 30 minutes, which was followed by sharp questions from four other committee members. As the chair of the committee, I had

Ajou Reporters at Stanford Univ. 2001

presided over the session of questions and answers for more than an hour and asked Kim, students and guests in the audience to leave the room, so we could decide the fate of the defender behind closed doors.

It took another 30 minutes until I opened the door, and said to Kim, "Congratulations Dr. Kim! The committee approved your dissertation." If he had not passed the defense, the Chair of the committee would call him Mr. Kim, which would cause any candidate to collapse. I was so proud of Dr. Kim, who did wonderful research in order to receive his doctoral degree while he was on leave from the Korean Broadcasting System in Korea. He returned to KBS and worked for a while, but later moved to the University of Colorado as a broadcasting professor.

Ajou Reporters in the Yosemite Park   2001

Upon the successful completion of Dr. Kim's degree, we were invited to the House of Chow for a big celebration. E.K. Park, however, kept pretty quiet until she asked a question that bothered her quite a bit. "Why did the closed committee meeting take so long? Were there any problems with Kim's defense?" I smiled at her and told her that we were just talking about campus gossip, and there was no problem with Kim's work. She could not believe that faculty members could just talk about insignificant subjects while the candidate was on the verge of a nervous breakdown waiting for it to end. I then explained that I had had my own defense just like that, and it seemed like an American tradition at dissertation defenses.

After the short but intensive journalism educational tour in Missouri, I divided the team into two groups: The first group of three reporters headed by C.K. Park would go to Gainesville, Florida, to report how incoming freshmen who were selected by their high scores of admission review would receive instruction in intensive English at the University of Florida. This was a

Yosemite Park   2001

first trial event for Ajou University to attract a talented freshman class. The second team was led by me with the new editor Kwon, and reporters Jung, Yoon and E.K. Park, who would travel to San Francisco to visit and report about Stanford University.

The first team reported to me that they had many difficulties in moving around the university town since nobody on the team knew how to drive. But they did their reporting and enjoyed the warm weather in Florida in February. My team did not have any logistical problem. We rented a car at the airport and drove to Stanford University the next day. I already had asked the students to prepare for their reporting assignment when we were in Suwon, and they knew what they were looking for. I had asked Ajou students to interview Stanford students and visit the library, a number of research institutes, and the student newspaper and student organizations. I did not go with them to help.

What they told me during the dinner in San Francisco's China Town was good enough for their first overseas reporting trip. I suggested a number of angles for their stories in our newspaper. I took them to a genuine Chinese gourmet restaurant that had been famous for a long time with a warning that they might not like it, since what they knew about Chinese food was a Korean version.

On the following day, we visited the University of California at Berkeley and did what we had done in Stanford University. We finished our work in the morning and took a tour bus to see the Golden Gate Bridge, Twin Peaks and downtown streets before we went into a Korean restaurant late in the evening. I was wondering what to do for the remaining last day in San Francisco and asked folks in the restaurant for suggestions. The owner suggested that we go to the Yosemite National Park, which should be open if the weather permitted. He called the park service to find out conditions for the next day and was told it should be okay for us to visit the following day.

I had been to the natural wonder of Yosemite a few times, but I never thought we would be able to go there in winter. Looking carefully on the map, it was a five-hour drive on the rugged terrain of the Rocky Mountains, where snow and ice were unavoidable during winter time. We actually had only one day to visit and needed to make sure we came back to the motel by night to catch the flight to Seoul. It was a bit risky, but we left for Yosemite around four in the morning.

As soon as we cleared the metro area, we were on the mountain highway, which was cleanly cleared with snow piling up on both sides like fences, and the scenery along the highway was just breathtakingly beautiful. We were so grateful to have this opportunity. When we arrived at the park, there were quite a few tourists who were wondering around. We took our time to see the park, but we could not stay there too long. We all agreed that we would come back here again in the future. We left the park and got back to the motel near the airport. We kept singing the song, "I left my heart in San Francisco...."

MT Retreat in Hong-Chon (2002): MT (Members Training) is a version of an orientation retreat, where new members were to be introduced and oriented to the organization, so that they would work better as a team. I was told that the original idea of MT was first introduced by a Japanese corporation and that activities of MT involved heavy drinking, excessive physical exercise, screaming, and so on. MT retreats had spread to Korean business corporations, and many college students adopted this for their extracurricular organizations. The best part of MT is that it is usually held in exotic remote resort areas, and members would be delighted to take a trip with friends.

E.K. Park was selected as the new editor of the campus newspaper, and she recruited six freshman reporters from many applicants. The new reporters were excited about working for the campus newspaper and going on the overseas reporting trip. Before the first semester in March, Park planned a MT trip to Hong-chon, where the Dae-myung resort establishment is located. Our university did not have a membership, but a new reporter, Choi, had her

father's membership, which allowed us to enjoy a one-night and two-day package. Dae-myung had arranged transportation and two big rooms for us.

College MTs normally would not take any faculty member, but E.K. Park persuaded me to join them. I was not sure what to expect, but I took it as a vacation trip to a remote mountainous town, where I had spent some time for my military service in 1959. On a bright sunny February day, we were gathered in Jamsil Sports Arena to board the DM bus to Hong-chon. The bus was packed with about 45 people, who carried a lot of food and drinks for the resort picnic. Because of the improved roads it only took a little more than two hours to reach the resort area while it used to take me all day to reach the same location in the 1950s.

Around lunch hour, we arrived at the luxury DM resort, which was located in a valley of the mountainous area of the Kang-won province. The complex included huge hotels, suites, many restaurants, a skiing area, which was converted to a nine hole golf course during non-snow season, lakes with row boats, a huge indoor sports building, where there were bowling lanes, billiard tables, ping pong tables, and many other sporting facilities. We all spent the whole afternoon trying out everything available for us and had a big dinner at the Korean restaurant. I became one of those young college students and participated in activities of young people, who did not seem to have had much experience in sports.

The real session of MT started after the dinner when we gathered in a large room with beer, whiskey, chips and fruit. I became the discussion leader on various subjects, including journalism, career, nationalism, global trends and even personal matters like marriage. We drank quite a bit of alcohol and continued rather serious discussions way after midnight, and we cooked Ramyun as a midnight snack. Our discussions were very serious and frank, and I learned a lot from the discussions about these young college students, who would not dare to say such things anywhere else.

As planned, we all got up early around six and went hiking in the rugged mountains for three hours. We had a good lunch at a restaurant and boarded the returning bus back to Seoul. We were tired from a busy program, but our brains were active while riding the bus. Nobody in our group was talking or sleeping. They were in deep thought. I really liked the MT concept, and I encouraged them to organize more such trips. But I told them I would not go with them anymore. It was a good experience for me as well as for them, but it could be different and better without faculty.

The Second Reporting Trip (2003): The second trip to the United States was organized in 2003 by J.S. Whang, a new editor and S.K. Kim, the administrative officer of the paper. Five reporters were to cover Harvard, Yale, Columbia and New York State at Stony Brook. were scheduled. This reporting plan was developed in advance so that the students could prepare for their reporting. I assigned the students to gather information about the universities that we were going to visit and made some appointments with key persons for our interview. But our reporters did not do their homework as I had expected and had to work hard to come up with stories about Harvard and Yale and American students.

The Korean school year starts in March and has a long winter break while summer break is shorter. I had already left Korea for Missouri right before Christmas and was waiting for their arrival in St. Louis on February 28, 2002. They went through a one-day orientation program by a Korean professor from Missouri.

We were very fortunate to have Dr. T.C. Jung, a professor of Kyungsung University in Busan. He was on his sabbatical leave at Missouri and explained to Ajou students how journalism education works at Missouri. Dr. Jung, a graduate of Missouri who was working on his newspaper design book during his leave, even arranged for the students to see the Columbia Missourian budget meeting where editors decide which stories should go to the front page and how to fill up news holes of the day.

After the Missouri orientation, we had to cover NY State University at Stony Brook first. Dr. Kim had been appointed as the Minister of Education in 2002, and Dr. Myung Oh was Ajou University President, who was a graduate of the NY State University and was named an endowed cCair of Electrical Engineering. We developed a joint program for five years to grant two degrees to students. It was the first time that Ajou students were to get an American degree in addition to a Korean degree. The program was widely publicized in Korea, and we just needed to do our reporting for our university. During our stay in New York, K.J. Kim, MBC correspondent in New York, helped us cover the university and showed us around New York City.

Harvard University

We had a series of great reporting on Harvard University. We attracted more talented students, who would work for the newspaper. One other plan I had was to turn our radio station into a television station, which would develop programs to be aired on our closed circuit and on our local cable network. I wish I had been a bit younger to take on such ambitious work, but I was too tired to complete the project.

Korea has a mandatory retirement law that allows university professors to teach until the age of 65 while secondary school teachers are forced to retire at 62. Government officials are required to retire when they are even younger than 62. I reached my limit in 2002 when I celebrated my 65th birthday, but the University rehired me for one more year. There was a discussion to extend my appointment, but I turned down the offer. I wanted to retire in Missouri in the fall of 2003. I had been thinking about my retirement plan for a long time, and I had many plans to enjoy my retirement.

Part IV
Retirement

Laguna Woods Village Golf Ptactice Range

I have settled in a retirement community, Laguna Woods Village in California. I work as a leader of a traveling group of retirees and am traveling around the world, searching for renewed meaning to my life in retirement. I also have been reading many books, both fiction and non-fiction, which I could not do when I was immersed in my academic research and teaching. I am also enjoying the natural wonders of the surrounding mountains and beaches and practicing my favorite sports, golf and fishing.

This painting above was drawn by an artist in Jefferson City, Missouri as a retirement gift by the Advertising Faculty in 2000.

The Village is about six miles east of Laguna Beach, but the ocean humidity is kept at bay by the surrounding hills, which is a boon for residents with arthritis. It takes only ten minutes to reach the beautiful sandy beach, and Young and I walk on the beach every Thursday. It's great exercise to walk on the soft sand while listening to the waves in the early morning. I often look over the horizon as we walk and wonder how far it is to the Korean peninsula.

Laguna Beach is the best preserved natural wonder on the coast of Southern California, yet Newport Beach, on the north side of the busy harbor, is one of the most developed and expensive, just a half-hour drive away. Dana Point also provides ocean fishing facilities. I've gone ocean fishing a few times. It costs $25 for an all-day trip, accompanied by about thirty other fishing enthusiasts. We've also driven to Jalama Beach for surf fishing or to Eastern Sequoia to fish for trout.

The Village is also a five-hour drive from 11,000-foot Mammoth Mountain, central California's favorite mountain resort on the eastern slope of the Sierra Nevada mountain range. Mammoth is a four-season destination resort with world-class facilities, lodging, and services. We love the beautiful scenery along the way whenever we drive there.

Nestled in the rolling foothills of Palomar Mountain, the historic Warner Springs Ranch resort is within a two-hour drive. It was established in 1844 and has been serving up western hospitality to travelers since the days of the Butterfield Overland Stage Coach. Today the resort is open to the public, offering package tours and serving the community in the finest tradition of a private club. There are 240 rustic-but-cozy cottages, most of them with fireplaces and mini-refrigerators, but without the intrusion of televisions or phones. It's an ideal spot to relax, to play, or to get reenergized.

The beautifully maintained golf course meanders through the western foothills of San Diego's Cuyamaca Mountains at an elevation of 3,000 feet. Picturesque mountain vistas and open grazing lands create the backdrop for a course that provides a superb challenge for golfers of any caliber.

In 1795, a Spanish expedition, led by Fray Juan Mariner, visited a beautiful valley in the San Jacinto Mountains in what is now Southern California. Besides the majestic grandeur, the adventurers were struck by a remarkable phenomenon they named Agua Caliente, hot mineral springs that would one day lure visitors from all over the world to that enchanted place.

Native Americans in the area used the natural pools of hot water for generations before settlers discovered Agua Caliente. Visitors found the hot mineral water invigorating and therapeutic, and weary travelers found respite and sustenance at the Warner Springs Ranch trading post. Those early travelers were the first to enjoy bathing in the hot springs, which would later make Warner Springs Ranch world famous.

In 1911, Warner Springs Ranch was purchased by William G. Henshaw, who built Lake Henshaw, a reservoir to keep pace with the increasing thirst of the growing area. The reservoir has become a major water source for metropolitan San Diego. New hot spring pools were constructed in 1922, and a golf course, dining room, and dance hall were added in 1945. Throughout its history, however, Warner Springs Ranch has retained its idyllic beauty, making it one of the world's most nature-blessed places.

1. Laguna Woods Village

Young and I really enjoy our retirement community. The city of Laguna Woods is home to the Laguna Woods Village, an independent-living community covering 3.8 square miles.

It has 12,736 dwellings and a population of about 18,000. The village has a twenty-seven-hole golf course right in the center and we can ride our golf cart from our home to the course or anywhere else in the Village. Golf carts are more important than cars here. We even do our basic shopping with our electric cart, which saves money on gasoline.

There are three types of ownership of housing: co-ops, condominiums, and care-giving tower units. Co-op living includes everything, even repair and maintenance by the management. Condos provide a bit more luxury, but require paying for repairs and maintenance. Tower living is for folks who are no longer able to cook or take care of themselves.

Laguna Woods Village   #2 Swimming Pool

This economically diverse community contains ninety-five styles of housing, ranging from studio apartments to three-bedroom freestanding homes. Prices currently range from $100,000 to $1.2 million. The average age of the Village is 78, and I'm one of the younger residents. It's widely said that if you can't live to 100 in this community, you've done something wrong, because it has everything you need to live a good, healthy, and long life.

There are two notable residents. The first is a former UC Irvine professor who won the Nobel Prize in chemistry in 2005. He still works in his lab and lives in a modest co-op unit. The second is Louis Wiseman, who was named Nonagenarian of 2006. Louis retired in 1986, but still plays the violin in the Village music group and is an avid world traveler. We also have a growing number of Korean-American residents, including a number of retired professors, physicians, and businessmen, all with the same goal: enjoying their retirement.

The city has the highest hospital density in the region and averages only three to five minutes in emergency response time. Since the Village has a limit of fifty-five or older, there is no need for a school. There are fourteen gates to the community and security guards patrol the area, so we can go out of town without having to worry about our home.

Many residents tend flower or vegetable gardens, and there are two garden centers. We rent a tree plot, where we have four orange trees and two plots of vegetables. Last year, we harvested so many squash that we were able to share them with our neighbors. This year, we grew a lot of Korean red peppers and we're drying them to make powder.

There are five swimming pools in town with varying water temperatures and facilities for swimming lessons and water ballet. One pool is open until 10:00 at night. The pool water is maintained with salt instead of chlorine.

The Village has two fitness centers with advanced equipment and a professional staff. There are also many classes and clubs providing a variety of social and learning experiences. Saddleback College Emeritus Program even offers more than 100 courses on-site.

For socializing, seven clubhouses are teaming with special interest groups. You'd be hard-pressed to find a group that isn't represented. We have a Korean-American club that includes a golf club, a ladies vocal group, and a Thursday night sports dance group. People here are active, both intellectually and physically.

In my mind, the best part is the weather. I know of no other town where the weather is as good year round as it is here. Before my retirement, I was often told that the Village was the best retirement town, but I didn't believe it until we moved here in February 2004. Since then, I've referred to the Village as "heaven on earth," and we've enjoyed living here ever since.

Publication Party

The publication of my first book after retirement, *Retirement without Retiring* in Korea was one the hardest ventures I ever undertook. I didn't know that no Korean publisher would want to handle such a book, because Koreans only bought textbooks or how-to books. Printing costs had also risen significantly, and many Korean publishers were having their books printed outside the country.

My book venture was being supported by $5,000 from the Bang Il-Young Foundation of the Chosun Ilbo, and such support had been more than enough for my previous books, but it wasn't enough at that time. In March 2007, I found a publisher who was new to the business, but he faced difficulties of his own trying to print my book, having to cut out many pictures and to implement several other cost-saving measures. I wasn't happy about it, but I finally accepted the situation and gave my approval—after a delay of six months.

The book was a collection of stories about retirement attitudes and activities, based on the Q methodology research technique developed in 1935 by Dr. William Stephenson, who had taught at the MU journalism school. I

collected many statements about retirement and selected thirty for the book, which were then factor analyzed and then divided into three types of retirement. Among the three types, the first was "retirement without retiring," illustrated by retiree stories, including my own.

As the publisher warned, the book wasn't going to be a best-seller in the Korean market, but residents in Laguna Woods Village were delighted. Some of our friends bought multiple copies and sent them as gifts to others in order to describe their retired life.

A women's group known as the "High Class Group" even hosted a gala to celebrate my book's publication. The party was attended by eighty people in black ties and evening gowns at 5:30 on November 11, 2007 in the main dining hall of Club House Seven.

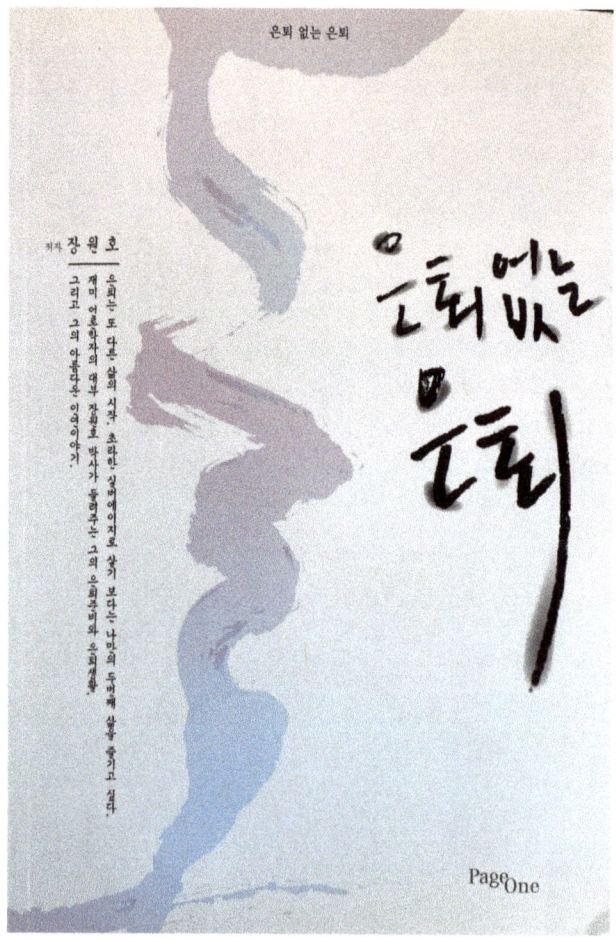

Phillip Shin, the master of ceremonies, opened up the ceremony with a toast to the joy of our lives together, which was followed by a prayer by Mr. Keun Young Yoo. Dinner was then served by Yolanda, with salmon, chicken, and steak.

After dinner, Thomas Koh told the gathering that he had found the book interesting, then said that he wanted to hear more of my thoughts on the relationship between "I and Thou." Mrs. Dukhee Lee, president of the Korean-American Club, also made congratulatory remarks, but the most fun part of the celebration was when I was roasted by Young Jin Hong, president of the Korean Golf Club, and Joseph Choi, who went into great detail about my lack of skill as a golfer and even greater lack of skill as a gentleman.

2. Golf and Retirement

Laguna Woods Village   Golf Course #2-1

"Golf is a game for a lifetime," says Mike Yoon, a retired orthopedic surgeon. "Golf gives me the enjoyment of playing with my lifelong partner, my wife, whenever she and I feel like playing. It seems the best way to catch up with our life together after retirement," says K.T. Hahn, a retired math professor from Penn State University.

Haesley 9 Bridge Golf Course

However, one golfer from Korea who plays every day here says he is saving about $300 every time he plays, which is the cost of a round in Korea. Even though he is willing to pay the high price in Korea, he doesn't get the tee times that he wants, nor can he find many friends able to join him.

"Golf is a game that can challenge your physical and mental capabilities," says Donna Oh, 2006 Women's Club champion. She further explains that golf can teach life lessons that can be applied to everyday life, such as patience, respect for others, strategic thinking, and honesty.

"Honesty is the key to golf," according to Peter Kim, who has played for more than 40 years. Peter told us a story that sounds very familiar to most of us. About four years ago, he was playing on the 12th hole and his second shot went over the green to the fence. He did not see anybody around, so he moved the ball from the fence to make it to the green. After that, however, he felt so guilty about it that he could not do well for the rest of the game. He could not even sleep well that night and invited his friends the next morning to breakfast to confess the sin.

Phil Shin, a former golf instructor, suggests that golf requires a constant quest for perfect swings, the right equipment, and the right instruction that can help you meet your goals. Phil also says that the game requires one to adjust one's competitive spirit to different situations and environments. For those who have not yet started, think of the fun you will have with your family and friends when you take up the game of golf. Even if playing golf doesn't provide you with those kinds of wisdom, you might just find yourself enjoying this wonderful game.

Golf has been one of the major activities for the majority of Koreans as well as American friends in this community. Many play regularly, three or four times a week. I served as treasurer for two years for the Men's Club, which has 500 members, and have been actively involved in the activities of the club.

Golf and Korea: Golf was introduced to the Korean public in the 1960s and has become one of the most popular and prestigious sports among the Korean people. The Hanyang Country Club in Guenjari, a suburb of Seoul, was built in 1964 and the Taenung golf course at the Korean Military Academy opened in 1966. The Korean Golf Association was formed the same year.

Historical documents show that the first six-hole course was developed by British settlers in the Wonsan area in 1897. The second was created in Hyochang Park by the Chosun Hotel in 1921, but that course stayed open only two years, when the area was designated a government park. The first playable Guenjari course was opened in 1929, but that course was later turned into a children's park. Today there are 170 golf courses in the southern half of the Korean peninsula and the cost of membership in some of these clubs can be as much as $1 million American dollars.

We were fortunate to be invited by a former student to play a round at the prestigious Haesley Nine Bridges Golf Club, which has only 140 members, where only members and accompanying guests can play. Unlike on most other Korean courses, we didn't see many other players that day.

A club employee told us that they plan to make that course one of the top twenty-five in the world. It's already listed among the top 100. There were nine beautiful bridges on the eighteen-hole course, and the fairways were as manicured as the greens on most other courses. The huge clubhouse was also gorgeous.

Happy New Year 2020

Laguna Woods Village   Golf Course #2-1

Although a typical round of golf consist of eighteen holes, many courses have twenty-seven or even thirty-six. The Pacific Golf course in Karuizawa, Japan, has seventy-two holes, each named after a flower.

A round of twenty-one holes isn't common in the States, but it's very common in Korea. After playing eighteen holes on the course, golfers go to the nineteen hole, which is a public bath house, then to a twentieth hole at the club restaurant and cocktail lounge, and finally to the twenty-first hole, which is located in a karaoke bar where they drink and sing.

Most Korean golf courses are built on mountainsides where farming isn't feasible. When you play these mountain courses, you feel as if you've just completed a full-scale exercise regimen, even though some courses are equipped with elevators or escalators. After five hours of hiking and swinging clubs, you're looking forward to the nineteenth hole, where you can either take a quick shower or soak in a large tub with your friends.

All nineteen holes have three tubs: one is hot, with water temperature around 109 degrees; the second is just warm, with the thermostat set at 106 degrees; and the third is cold, with water at a chilly 60 degrees. You'll often find golfers switching back and forth between the hot and cold tubs after a round of golf. According to many experienced Korean golfers, switching between tubs aids blood circulation and prevents heart attacks.

A friendly round of golf isn't complete without the last three holes, according to Dr. Auh Ryung Lee, a professor emeritus of literature and comparative cultures, since eating and drinking together is the most important communication channel among Koreans, who wouldn't tell each other what's really on their minds during simple conversations.

Primm Valley Golf Tour: The Men's Golf Club and my wife Young's Women's Golf Club have been organizing a number of trips to play golf. During the holidays of December 2008, the Men's Club organized a two-day field trip to Primm Valley for two rounds of golf at the Primm Valley golf course. Seventy-four people gathered at 8:00 in the morning on the second day of December 2008 and boarded two buses. We were all as excited as grade school kids when we used to take field trips twice a year.

Most of my childhood field trips did not provide any transportation and we would walk several miles to some scenic places. We did not have candies or picnic food. We all carried our lunch boxes of steamed rice and seasoned vegetables with pan-fried anchovies. The best treats were hard-boiled eggs and some fruit, like apples or pears. It was the second half of the 1940s, after the end of the Second World War. We were all very poor.

Haesley 9 Bridge Golf Course
Magnificent Club House
2012

After a lunch stopover in Barstow, our golf group arrived in Primm Valley a bit earlier than scheduled and found that we seemed to have arrived in a ghost town where we did not see many people or cars. As we were in a recession, we felt the economic slump as a result of the recession. The casino hotel, Whiskey Peter, had only a skeleton crew for the basic operation, which was so terribly slow and inefficient that we had to wait an hour before we got checked into our rooms.

We had been to Las Vegas many times, but this was the first time I had ever complained to the management about bad service. As we checked into the room, I wanted to have ice cubes, which were supposed to be on my floor near the elevator. The ice machine did not work, and the ones on three other floors I checked did not work either. It was just terrible, which also is the name of the casino in Primm Valley, located close to the state border of California.

We had two free dinner coupons, but we had to take a shuttle bus to cross I-15 and wait a long time to get some service. I do not gamble. I had a

number of things to do in the hotel room. As usual, there were a few friends who bragged about winning money, but I do know what that winning really means.

The first day of the golf tournament was on the Lakes course, a gorgeous new design on the desert and maintained almost perfectly for amateur golfers. The first day format was an individual contest, and Young and I were assigned to play with Bud and Betty Kolstow, who had the highest handicap level among the players. I was honored to play with them and found out that Bud earned his doctoral degree from Iowa long before I did and retired from his teaching at ISU at Carbondale in 1965. He belongs to my father's generation but played well for his game. Young shot a 98, four over her handicap, and I shot an 86, which was my handicap for the day. I also won the closest to pin contest for the day.

The second day's play was on the Desert course for an individual contest with foursome based on the first day scores. I won the first day A flight with a net score of 71 and was assigned to the first group with Bob Howe (handicap 4), Ralph Belitz (6) and Peter Oh (14). I played well again and shot another 86, which was good enough to win second place.

However, I won the overall two-day contest with a net of 142 and was awarded $101, and Young got $62. She also won a Skin worth of $26 for the first day. It was a very rewarding trip for us as many people told me that they really liked my writing in The Globe, our community newspaper. We enjoyed our playing well on a very nice golf course.

Over the years, I had published many articles about the exotic aspects of golf in Far Eastern countries.

A shade house is located every four or five holes at most Korean golf clubs. Such a shade house with air-conditioning and heating offers drinks, food, comfortable chairs, wash rooms, and friendly waitresses who seem to know everything.

A shade house is almost a necessity in Korean golf to control the flow of players. Most clubs have 6-minute intervals in tee times and every golfer in Korea seems to be in a hurry. If you practice swing more than once, you get dirty looks. If you do so repeatedly, your caddy will issue you a warning. When you reach the shade house, you will find at least one or two foursomes drinking, eating, and chatting for a while. Some Japanese clubs have a one-hour break period after playing the first nine holes.

The shade houses are a haven for caddies, who have their own room where they can enjoy expensive drinks and food while the bills go to the golfers. As golf is supposed to be for the rich and famous, golfers cannot complain about the cost that sometimes can get very expensive. Each caddy gets about $80 as tips per round and each golfer chips in $20 when a foursome hires one caddy. It can get extremely expensive if your foursome hires more than one caddy.

Hiring a caddy is not an option at most golf clubs in Korea. When your foursome hires one caddy with an electric golf cart, you have to pay about $40 additionally for the cart. However, the caddy system in Korea is rapidly changing. Some clubs are offering the choice to drive your own cart.

About 20 years ago, I was required to hire three caddies for a round of golf in Thailand; one carried my golf bag, the second one carried an umbrella and folding chair for me, and the third one helped me choose the right clubs and washed my ball when I reached the greens. I recall it cost me $5 for each caddy at that time. Each foursome marched with a troop of 12 caddies.

Laguna Woods Village   Executive Courses

Typologies of Golfers: "Playing golf gives me great pleasure I love and the challenge of learning due to the complexity of the game."

This is just one of the 100 statements I received when I asked friends and golfers the reasons why they play golf. I am interested in developing typologies of golfers and am working with about 30 statements, which are sorted according to the likes and dislikes of my selected golfers. I am in the very early stage of this ambitious project, but I am finding very interesting aspects of different types of golfers.

"Recreational golfer" is the first type that has been developed from the responses. The majority of people who belong to this type are retirees. This type believes golf is a lifetime game. Golf means physical exercise, this type says, and you can enjoy playing in a beautiful outdoor environment of well-groomed grass, trees, and fresh air. They also strongly agree with the statement, "Golf is a game that can and will challenge your physical and mental capabilities." Playing golf requires total concentration and peacefulness, which is, of course, no easy task.

Haesley Nine Bridge Golf Course

One 75-year-old new golfer who was an excellent tennis player expressed his delight and frustration. He thought hitting a white ball on the tee should be easier than a flying tennis ball. He practices every day to meet the challenge of playing with the small white ball, in his belief that golf will provide him with the physical as well as the mental exercise he needs.

Playing golf will help the most impatient people, according to people of this type. While playing, your face twists and turns in every shot, and the game requires the golfer to adjust to different situations and environments. They also like the idea that golf offers opportunities to meet many interesting people and socialize with friends.

Another type developed is the "competitive golfer," to whom winning is every-thing. A large number of young Korean golfers, and possibly Tiger Woods him-self, belong to this type. One of the young LPGA golfers I met told me that she really wanted to go to college and take classes with friends. She said she had nev-er gone to any class since her junior high school.

Las Vegas Match Play: "Playing for a dollar a stroke makes me excited and as nervous as a professional golfer shivers with a short put for thousands of dollars," says Anthony Smith, who often visits and plays here. Anthony, with a seven handicap, would not play with us if there were no bet, at least a dollar on each stroke and "skin." Anthony is one of many golfers who were identified as a "competitive golfer" type in my study of golfer typologies.

Practice is an absolute requirement for the competitive golfer, who hits 320 range balls (four large buckets) every day in addition to his regular round of playing. Anthony also mentioned that Tiger Woods runs 5 miles with 75 pounds on his back before he practices with 1,500 balls every day. A competitive golfer gets satisfaction from winning money, his reward for hard work. The competitive golfer also stresses the strict abidance of rules and honesty.

Competitive golfers do not enjoy playing with high handicapped recreational golfers, but they opt for so-called "Las Vegas Match Play" when they do.

There are many versions of this game and one of the versions is as follows: Each player deposits 20 dollars and divides a foursome into two groups for the match play. The first drive shots identify the rank of the players, and the player with the best drive teams with the one who ends up the worst, while the second and third best form the other team. The winning twosome will take 2 dollars each on every hole.

The teams for the match for the second hole will be formed by the scores of the first hole. The players with the best score for the first hole and the worst scorer get to be new partners. If a hole ends in a tie, the prize money accumulates to the next hole with the same players on each team.

There are four extra awards that are placed as extra bets for the closest to the pin competition. It takes a bit of luck to win money, as it depends on who you are paired with. Usually, you still get back half of your deposit, even if you play badly. You may try this game just for the fun of it.

Perfect Golf Swing: "The perfect golf swing is a myth," says Leo Sung Pak, a long hitter among our club members. "All you have to do is to look at the variety of swings by professional golfers on television." Still, he adds, they do have some common elements. "They all start with good fundamentals: grip, aim, and setup, and the swing repeats itself exactly every time."

Nevertheless, a scientist claims to have found the secret to the perfect golf swing, and it's not "all in the wrists," as the popular adage goes. "The key is knowing at exactly what stage of the swing you should exert the maximum force," according to a British researcher, Robin Sharp, who published his study online on Nov. 5, 2009.

Based on a golfer's physical dimensions and strengths, and using the top -of-the-back-swing position, Sharp has calculated how to achieve the maximum club-head speed for a standard driver upon impact with the ball. Bernard Hunt's best swing is used as an example. The positions of the shoulders, arms, grips, and club shaft are shown at 10-

The model shows that Hunt's drive distance could have been improved by "increasing the shoulder torque quickly to the maximum value, and then maintaining it throughout the rest of the swing, while initially holding back with his arms and wrists." The timing of the switch from holding back to hitting through with the arms is the most critical feature of the swing.

"Generating too much arm speed too soon causes an early release," writes Sharp, "with the club-head reaching its maximum speed before it arrives at the ball. The optimal strategy consists of hitting first with the shoulders while holding back with arms and wrists and after some delay, hitting through with the arms."

At release, the timing of famous members. To join the club, you have to wait till a vacancy arises. Membership costs more than $1 million U. S. dollars, and the monthly dues cost $2,000. The clubhouse looks like a huge museum or theater with a gorgeous wooden design.

There were, of course, nine beautiful bridges on the eighteen-hole lay-out. I was most impressed with the fairways, which looked like the greens of other courses. However, we weren't allowed to drive our cart on the fairways, which meant I didn't enjoy it as much as I enjoy playing on our home course at Laguna Woods Village.

I wonder how many Korean golfers think golf is a game for the rich and famous. I still think golf is a game that can be enjoyed for a lifetime by anybody. The folks who live in the Village don't need to go to Pine Valley, Pebble Beach, St. Andrews to enjoy this wonderful game. which depends on the combination of shoulder and arm actions employed, the wrists should hit through. Breaking with conventional thinking, Sharp's study suggests that the wrists are

not as important as the way a golfer uses his or her arms. Knowing exactly how long that "delay" should last is the crucial factor.

His research also concludes that height is not as advantageous as previously thought, with short people able to hit a ball almost as far as their taller competitors if they use the right technique.

The perfect golf swing was figured out by Robin Sharp of England with his mechanical engineering background, but "golf is not a game of perfect," as the title of a book (Simon and Schuster, 1995) by Bob Rotella puts it. Rotella is the director of sports psychology at the University of Virginia and has been a consultant to including the PGA, the LPGA and the senior LPGA.

"On the first tee, a golfer must expect only two things of himself: to have fun and to focus his mind properly on every shot," Rotella says. "Golfers must learn to love a challenge when they hit a ball into the roughs, trees, or sand. The alternatives—anger, fear, whining,and cheating—do no good. Confidence is critical to good golf. Confidence is simply the aggregate of the thoughts you have of yourself. It is more important to be decisivethan to be correct when preparing to play any golf shot or put."

Happy New Year 2018

January 7, 2018

One of my friends who carries an 18-handicap and is known as a perpetual complainer, missed a short putt on the first hole after making an unusual second shot to land on the green. He whined and screamed all the way to the 18th hole and had another round of bad golf. When we were chatting in the lounge after the game, the perpetual complainer was advised to read Rotella's book.

A statistician friend among the foursome also explained the normal distribution of putts. When you putt so many times, you may make as many difficult putts as you may miss easy putts, about 16 percent of the time. The complainer should have thought that the first hole was a par 5 for him and should, therefore, be delighted to have made his par on the hole.

Another friend suggested he read Zen Golf: Mastering the Mental Game (Doubleday, 2002) by Joseph Parent, who is a noted PGA instructor and taught Buddhist philosophy and stress reduction methods for more than 25 years. "Great golf comes from confidence and concentration, the ability to stay in the present and block out distraction," the Buddhist follower writes. "Achieving a clear mind is also the heart of Buddhist philosophy and practice." However, he was also advised not to meditate while he was playing the game.

2

Golf and Humor: "You have to be very strict about the rules for yourself but should be very generous to other players," says Yong Paik, who is known as one of the best partners to play with in the Village. He emphasizes that golf is meant to be enjoyed, even though improving your skill and scores are also an important part of the game.

Yong always brings new humorous jokes to the game, which entertains almost every player. As a former CEO of Samsung Finance in Korea, he has plenty of humor about golf and knowledge of good dishes and restaurants that put other players in a friendly mood so as to enjoy the game.

"Your drive shot is an inherited asset from your parents, but iron shots and putting are your own. Good and long drive shots do not guarantee you good rounds of golf. You need to manage properly with irons and the putter, just like you manage your life.

There are so many roughs, hazards, trees, sand traps, and hilly greens on the golf course; as many as 108 types of hindrances and obstacles in life as symbolized in a string of Buddhist beads that must be overcome on the path to enlightenment."

Cabo San Lucas

Although a devoted Christian, Yong uses the basic philosophy of Buddhism to explain similarities between playing golf and managing life, and emphasizes the importance of our efforts to improve both the game of golf and life.

Yong also introduced us to a restaurant in the Tustin area where good sashimi and fish plates are served. The exotic place also serves blowfish, which is known to carry a deadly poison in its blood and eggs, and the restaurant needed to have a special license to serve the fish. We were told the fish were imported from Argentina rather than from Japan and Korea, where such fish are known as a rare delicacy and very expensive. Many of us who visited the restaurant enjoyed the special soup with the blowfish. So far, I have not heard of anyone dying from poisonous blowfish.

When I find golfers arguing and screaming at each other on the course, I wonder how much fun they are missing out on, as the oriental philosopher observed. We all need a compassionately caring attitude toward friends as we play golf and live our lives.

Golf and Self Esteem: "One of the reasons I play golf is that the game helps me to enhance my self-esteem and to develop a sense of perseverance and patience. Golf is not a game that needs to be perfected in order to be enjoyed. I still get frustrated by the same mistakes I make again and again. However, I feel better about myself through this wonderful game and improve my sense of self-worth." So explains Dr. Harry Kim, a retired psychiatrist, who plays the golf every day as long as the weather permits.

I am not so sure that I am motivated to enhance my self esteem as much, but I love to play the game on different courses. I played our pro-am tournament in November last year with Leo Pak and his wife, and our pro was Rod Linville, the manager and pro of the Encinitas Ranch Golf Club, who invited us to play at his golf course. The Paks, Young, my wife, and I went down to the course in December last year. The course is located on a hill, from where we could see the Pacific Ocean and feel the nice breeze from the water.

Haesley Nine Bridges Golf Club

Encinitas Ranch is carved from former poinsettia flower fields on magnificent bluffs overlooking the Pacific. The design incorporates dramatic elevation changes to add excitement to an already challenging championship course that has been a qualifying site for the PGA Tour's Buick Invitational.

Encinitas Ranch Golf Club was developed some time ago when the beautiful scenic ranch was perfect for the housing and golf course, but a stressful downturn in housing developments in southern California came sooner than they had expected, and there seemed to be many vacant lots to be filled. However, the golf course was gorgeous and playing there would stretch you, as each game is filled with problems to be solved, just like our life! Get out there and enjoy it!

American golf courses make money from the housing developments around the golf course while earnings from the management of the golf playing has been decreasing to the point where profits became very difficult to make, according to a manager of the Pelican Hill Resort and Golf, which is in a very difficult financial situation.

Charlie Chaplin and Golf: A sad-faced gentleman walked into a psychiatrist's office, wanting to know how to be happy. The doctor told him to go see a performance by Charlie Chaplin, who was sure to make him laugh and cheer him up. The sad-faced man replied, "I am Charlie Chaplin."

Sir Charles Spencer, aka Charlie Chaplin, an English comic actor and film director of the silent film era, left many memorable and enjoyable stories about his life. One of the most remarkable quotes of Charlie Chaplin is, "Life is a tragedy when seen in close-up, but a comedy in long-shot." This paradoxical statement has been used in many different respects, including in one's approach to golf.

I repeated to my friends that "golf is a tragedy when seen in close-up, but a comedy in long-shot." Then I received the following paradoxical poem from Dr. Charles Kim, a retired professor of mathematics. I'm not sure who the author is, but it is worth quoting.

My life has not been quite the same, since I chose to play this stupid game. It rules my mind for hours on end, a fortune it has made me spend. It has made me curse and made me cry, hate myself and want to die.

"It promises a thing called par, if I hit it straight and far. To master such a tiny ball should not be very hard at all. But the ball refuses my desires, and does exactly as it chooses. It hooks and slices, dribbles and dies, and disappears before my eyes. Often it will have a whim to hit a tree or take a swim.

"With miles of grass on which to land, it finds a tiny patch of sand. Then it has me offering up my soul, if only it would find the hole. It's made me whimper like a pup, and I swear I will give up. And take to drink to ease my sorrow, but the ball knows I will be back tomorrow."

A recent study found the average golfer walks about 900 miles a year. Another study found golfers drink, on average, 22 gallons of alcohol a year. That means, on average, golfers get about 41 miles to the gallon. Kind of make you proud. Almost feel like a hybrid.

Golf, however, is neither a tragedy nor a comedy. It is an enjoyable game for a lifetime for me.

The best golf course in the world has been New Jersey Pine Valley, followed by Cypress Point of Pebble Beach, Augusta National, St. Andrews in Scotland, and Royal County Down of Northern Island, according to www.golf.com/top-courses.

The rankings used to be guided by a panel of 100 members, representing fifteen countries. The men and women who cast votes included major-championship winners, Ryder Cup players, architects, amateurs, journalists, and a cadre of nearly a dozen course connoisseurs who've played all Top 100 Courses in the World. However, in 2007, the ranking organization switched to a web-based system that allowed panelists to vote on a combined master list of 475 courses from around the world. Panelists can only vote for courses they've played. On average, each panelist had played seventy-three courses on the Top 100 list.

I've played many exotic courses in the world, but none of them made any notable ranking, except for the Nine Bridges in Jeju Island of South Korea, which was ranked the 55th. In 2010, I had an opportunity to play the second Nine Bridges in the suburb of Seoul and was told that the course is expected to be in the top 25 in the near future.

Haesley Nine Bridges Golf Club in Korea has only 140 rich and famous members. To join the club, you have to wait till a vacancy arises. Membership costs more than $1 million U. S. dollars, and the monthly dues cost $2,000. The clubhouse looks like a huge museum or theater with a gorgeous wooden design.

There were, of course, nine beautiful bridges on the eighteen-hole layout. I was most impressed with the fairways, which looked like the greens of other courses. However, we weren't allowed to drive our cart on the fairways, which meant I didn't enjoy it as much as I enjoy playing on our home course at Laguna Woods Village.

I wonder how many Korean golfers think golf is a game only for the rich and famous. I still think golf is a game that can be enjoyed for a lifetime by anybody. The folks who live in the Village don't need to go to Pine Valley, Pebble Beach, St. Andrews to enjoy this wonderful game.

3. Traveling

Rangiroa 섬의 Kia Ora 호텔 앞에서 (2014년 2월 10일)

A. Greece

B. Turkey

C. Laos

D. Hong Kong

Traveling and writing stories about exotic places are one of major activities of our retirement living in our retirement community. Two books about our traveling were written and published.

The these books are available for reading on my personal website: **whchang.tistory.com.**

Cruising Stories2

CRUISING
Stories2

Won Ho Chang

Prologue

I was once told by my grandfather that my life's destiny came under the sign of the "running horse," and that destiny would one day carry me around the world. The Confucian source of that prophecy, *The Book of Changes*, considered one person's lifespan to be sixty years.

I've now surpassed that span by more than two decades, but my destiny keeps me running. Now, as a retiree, I've settled at Laguna Woods Village, in California, but I will continue to travel the world and search for renewed meaning in my life.

What meaning does my life hold for me now? I invite you to join me as I run to explore that question in the pages that follow.

장원호 여행기

난, 한국이 좋다

Korean Book Club

난, 한국이 좋다

나는 사주팔자에 역마살이 끼어있는 모양이다. 세 살 때 부모와 떨어져 조부모와 같이 살면서 할아버지로부터 한자와 예절을 배우며 유학을 시작했다. 이어 청주, 서울을 거쳐, 미국 유학 생활까지 이어졌고, 그 타향살이는 아직도 미국에서 계속 중이다.

미국의 대학교수는 정년이 없다. 일부 미국 교수들은 70세에 은퇴하지만, 많은 미국 교수들은 대개 65세에 은퇴한다. 나는 63세에 미국 교수직을 은퇴하고, 서울에 가서 아주대학교에서 다시 석좌교수로 3년을 보낸 뒤, 결국 66세에 은퇴했다. 당시, 아주대학교에서 좀더 있으라고도 했으나, 나는 단호히 교직을 떠났다. 그 이유는 은퇴하고 난 뒤 골프도 치고 싶었고, 특히 여행하면서 글을 쓰려는 계획이 있었기 때문이었다.

A. Greece

The Olympic Torch from Athens to London

Our trip to holy places in Greece and Turkey was organized by twelve friends of the Laguna Woods Village after a considerable study of the area. We chose to tour by ground transportation instead of cruising by ship to the surrounding ports. It was logistically easier to visit the areas.

We landed in Athens, the capital of Greece and the birthplace of the Olympic Games, democracy, and Western philosophy. As we were traveling from the new airport to the central part of this historical city on May 16, 2012, we were told by a Korean tour guide that "people here are very proud of their history, but they need a national determination to develop economically." Greece is in a terrible financial dilemma and their leaders were thinking about moving out of euro dollars, since the country wasn't ready to par with developed countries such as Germany and France.

The first place we visited was the Olympic stadium, where the final rehearsal for sending the Olympic Torch from Athens to London was going on. The official ceremony would be held the next day. We were pleased to see the Korean national flag displayed in honor of hosting of the 1988 Games—one of nine flags from countries that had recently hosted the Olympics.

However, there is increasing criticism that the Olympics may no longer serve longer the original objectives and spirit, which were to promote peace and harmony among nations through sports. Like many other international competitions, the Olympic Games have become commercial events, offering monetary gain and exploiting athletes according to race, gender, or even religious beliefs.

The Parthenon and Democracy

The Parthenon was amazing, since it was an important part of the great history of Greece more than 2,500 years ago, when other parts of the world were dominated by kings and queens, who built castles and lived luxurious lives at the expense of their subjects.

The Parthenon is an enduring symbol of Ancient Greece and the Athenian democracy, which developed around 508 B.C. Greece remains a unique and intriguing experiment in direct democracy, a political system in which the people don't elect representatives to vote on their behalf but vote on legislation themselves.

As a member of the freshman class of Political Science at Korea University in 1957, I had heard lectures about various political systems, and Athenian democracy was one of the first items on that list. After fifty-five years, I was finally looking at the actual historical monument I had heard about.

The Parthenon was originally constructed as a temple dedicated to the Greek goddess Athena, whom the people of Athens considered to be their virgin patron. Its construction began in 447 B.C., when the Athenian Empire was at the height of its power. It was completed in 432 B.C.

The Areopagus

It is the most important surviving building of Classical Greece, generally considered to be the culmination of the development of the Doric order. Its decorative sculptures were some of the highest points of Greek art.

Like most Greek temples, the Parthenon was also used as a treasury. For a time, it served as the treasury of the Delian League, which later became the Athenian Empire. In the fifth century A.D., the Parthenon was converted into a Christian church dedicated to the Virgin Mary.

After the Ottoman conquest, the Parthenon was turned into a mosque in 1460 and had a minaret built onto it. But Ottoman ammunition in the building was later ignited by a Venetian bombardment. The resulting explosion severely damaged the Parthenon and its sculptures. However, it remains a magnificent monument to the history of mankind.

The Areopagus is located between the Agora and the Acropolis. During the monarchical period, the college of the state Supreme Court was presided over by the King, but around 624 B.C., that power transferred to an assembly of elders (former rulers). Its main function was to deal with the violation of laws and blood crimes. Its membership consisted of members of the aristocracy, through seniority or hereditary. However, the Areopagus lost control of public life with the rise of democracy and began to decline after 487 B.C.

The Prison of Socrates

Philosophy

In the sixth century B.C., Greece was the origin of a number of Western philosophical traditions. The first philosophers were called "Pre-Socratic," which indicates that they developed before the time of Socrates. The Pre-Socratic philosophers came from various Greek colonies, and only fragments of their original teachings survive.

A new period of philosophy started with Socrates (469 – 399 B.C.), who rejected *the physical speculations* his predecessors had indulged in and made the *thoughts and opinions* of people his starting point. The teachings of Socrates were compiled by Plato, who combined them with many of the principles established by earlier philosophers and then developed the material into a comprehensive system.

Aristotle of Stagira, the most important disciple of Plato, shared the title of the greatest philosopher of antiquity with his teacher, but while Plato had sought to elucidate and explain things from the supra-sensual standpoint, Aristotle preferred to start from the facts people learn by experience. Other schools of Greek philosophy included Stoicism, Skepticism, Neo-Platonism, and Epicureanism.

Tucked away and little noticed in Athens is the Prison of Socrates. Located on the Philopappou Hill, home to the monument of Philopappus at the summit, is a set of caves—many with bars on them. Popular tradition says that this was where Socrates was held and where he was forced to drink the hemlock that killed him.

Through his portrayal in Plato's dialogues, Socrates has become renowned for his contribution to the field of ethics, and it is this Platonic Socrates that lends his name to the concepts of Socratic irony and the Socratic Method, or *elenchus*. The latter remains a commonly used tool in a wide range of discussions and is a type of pedagogy in which a series of questions are asked, not only to draw individual answers, but also to encourage fundamental insight into the issue at hand.

It is Plato's Socrates that also made important and lasting contributions to the fields of epistemology and logic, and the influence of his ideas and approach remains strong in providing a foundation for much of the Western philosophy that followed.

Meteora

Meteora's Ascetic Life

Our tour guide offered me a statement on religion, obtained from a religious scholar. "Religions claim that gods created humans, but humans created gods. The weakness of mankind against natural disaster, uncontrollable disease, and unattainable greed needed gods and religions to rely on, and human beings have tried to live under religious categories and rituals for thousands of years. Many martyrs even sacrificed their lives for their beliefs."

The Meteora is one of the largest and most important complexes of Eastern Orthodox monasteries in Greece, second only to Mount Athos. The six monasteries are built on natural sandstone rock pillars at the northwestern edge of the Plain of Thessaly near the Pineios River and Pindus Mountains in central Greece. The nearest town is Kalambaka. In the ninth century, an ascetic group of hermit monks moved to the ancient pinnacles. They were the first people to inhabit Meteora.

They lived in hollows and fissures in the rock towers, some of which reach 1,800 feet above the plain. This great height, combined with the sheerness of the cliff walls, kept away all but the most determined visitors. Initially the hermits led a life of solitude, meeting only on Sundays and special days to worship and pray in a chapel at the foot of a rock known as Dhoupiani.

The exact date of the establishment of the monasteries is unknown. By the late eleventh and early twelfth century, a rudimentary monastic group called the Skete of Stagoi was based in the still-standing church of Theotokos (Mother of God). By the end of the twelfth century, an ascetic community had blossomed in Meteora.

In 1344, Athanasios Koinovitis, from Mount Athos, brought a group of followers to Meteora. From 1356 to 1372, he founded the great Meteoran monastery at Broad Rock, which was perfect for the monks. They were safe from political upheaval and had complete control of the entry to their monastery. The only means of reaching it was by climbing a long ladder, which was drawn up whenever the monks felt threatened.

Corinth Canal

Saint Stephen Monastery

At the end of the fourteenth century, the Byzantine Empire's 800-year reign over northern Greece was being threatened by Turkish raiders who wanted control over the fertile plain of Thessaly. The hermit monks, seeking a retreat from the expanding Turkish occupation, found the inaccessible rock pillars of Meteora to be an ideal refuge. More than twenty monasteries were built, and six still remain today. There is a common belief that Athanasius (founder of the first monastery) didn't scale the rock but was carried there by an eagle.

Of the six remaining monasteries, four were inhabited by men and two by women. Each monastery has fewer than ten inhabitants currently. The monasteries are now tourist attractions.

Saint Paul

New Corinth was founded in 1858, after an earthquake destroyed the existing settlement that had developed in and around the site of ancient Corinth and its port, located north of the city center and close to the northwest entrance of the Corinth Canal, which serves the needs of industry and agriculture. It is mainly a cargo exporting facility.

The port of Corinth is an artificial harbor (approximately thirty feet deep), protected by a concrete mole. A new pier, finished in the late 1980s, doubled the capacity of the port. The reinforced mole protects anchored vessels from strong northern winds, and sea traffic is limited to trade in the export of local produce—mainly citrus fruits, grapes, marbles, aggregates, and some domestic imports.

We were looking for traces of Paul the Apostle, who was five years younger than Jesus and was perhaps the most influential early Christian missionary. The writings ascribed to him form a considerable portion of the New Testament. Paul's influence on Christian thinking was significant, due in part to his position as a prominent apostle during the spreading of the gospel in early Christian communities across the Roman Empire.

Paul was educated in Jerusalem in law and shipbuilding, which helped finance his missionary work. He also worked with church organizations, initiating moves, supervising the process, and rechecking projects by writing thoughtful religious letters.

Church Site of Philippi

According to the New Testament, Paul was known as Saul prior to his conversion and was dedicated to the persecution of the early disciples of Jesus in the area of Jerusalem. While traveling from Jerusalem to Damascus on a mission to "bring those which were there bound unto Jerusalem," the resurrected Jesus appeared to Saul. Saul was struck blind during that encounter, but after three days his sight was restored by Ananias of Damascus and Paul began to preach that Jesus of Nazareth was the Jewish Messiah and the Son of God.

Paul spent eighteen months in Corinth. The reference in the biblical book of Acts to proconsul Gallio helps ascertain that date. Paul met Aquila and Priscilla in Corinth. They became believers and helped Paul with his missionary journeys, following him to Ephesus, where they founded one of the strongest churches of that time. In 52 A.D., the missionaries sailed to Caesarea to greet the church there and then traveled north to Antioch, where they stayed for about a year before leaving on their third missionary journey.

In 49 or 50 A.D., Paul visited the city of Philippi during his second missionary journey. According to the book of Acts, he was guided there by a vision of "a man of Macedonia." Accompanied by Silas, Timotheus, and Luke, Paul preached in Philippi. The Jewish community there seems to have been small, but Paul and his friends found a group of Jewish women gathered at a river to the west of the city on the Sabbath. Paul baptized Lydia, a purple dye merchant, who invited the missionaries to stay at her home.

In another account recorded in Acts, Paul drove an evil spirit out of slave girl who had been working as a fortune-teller. Her owners became angry and dragged Paul and Silas into the marketplace, where they complained about them before the magistrates. A crowd joined in the condemnation and the missionaries were stripped and flogged, then thrown into prison.

At midnight, however, a great earthquake shook the earth and the prison doors flew open. The jailer nearly killed himself over the incident, but Paul talked him out of it and converted him. The next morning, the magistrates released Paul and Silas and ordered them to leave the city.

Paul visited Philippi on two other occasions, in 56 and 57 A.D. His epistle to the Philippians dates from around 54 A.D. and shows the immediate impact of Paul's preaching. The subsequent development of Christianity in Philippi is well documented, notably in a letter from Polycarp of Smyrna addressed to the community in Philippi around 160 A.D. and in various funerary inscriptions.

Saint Lidia's Baptistery

Lydia was baptized, along with her entire household, and Paul stayed at her home while living in Philippi. The Bible states: "Now a certain woman named Lydia heard us. She was a seller of purple, from the city of Thyatira, who worshipped God. The Lord opened her heart to heed the things spoken by Paul. And when she and her house were baptized, she begged us, saying, 'If you have judged me to be faithful to the Lord, come to my house and stay.' And she constrained us."

Lydia was a woman of great hospitality and faith. As a successful businesswoman, she most likely had a home spacious enough to welcome guests and to use as a Christian center where people could gather for the Holy Mass and prayer. After Paul and Silas were released from prison, they immediately went to Lydia's house to encourage the believers gathered there.

Our tour guide had a close friendship with the baptistery manager, who was waiting for us even after the regular closing hour. We had a friendly tour of that holy place and the manager later told us that his grandfather had fought in the Korean War.

After the visit to Lydia's Baptistery, which was the last agenda item on our tour in Greece, we checked into a modern hotel in Neopolis (Kavala), the seaport of the Philippi that was used by Paul. Our trip to Greece was a gratifying experience for me to look back on the cradle of Western civilization in relation to my own life.

I also came to realize what genuine pleasure in life is and am determined to develop a culture that balances both a healthy minds and a good physical conditions. Koreans of the past had developed a way of life through a harmonious state of mind derived from Confucius' teachings and Buddhist meditation. I need to revive that state of mind in order to have a genuinely pleasurable life as described by Epicurus.

B. Turkey

We were greeted by new tour guides, who helped us to move into another bus after crossing the border from Greece. A Turkish tour guide who spoke some Koreans was in charge of our tour program, but the actual guiding work was done by a Korean guide, who outlined our six-day agenda for touring the eastern half of Turkey.

We were scheduled to visit Troy, Ephesus, Pamukkale, Cappadocia, and Istanbul, and it would normally take two weeks to cover such a wide area. Our tour guide warned us our schedules would be tight. He said we'd get wake-up calls at six in the morning, eat a quick breakfast, and be on our way before eight. We'd also be walking long distances.

Eastside Bosphorus Strait and Blue Mosque

We crossed the Aegean Sea by ferry to Canakkale, Turkey, Asian extreme west. The eastern part is the Korean Peninsula. Some Korean political leaders used this geographical situation as the reason for calling Korea and Turkey "brother countries."

After a bumpy ride over rough highways, we stayed our first night in a seaside hotel near the ancient site of Troy. The hotel and area were so beautiful that I asked my friends to think about just staying there during the rest of the vacation.

Troy

Touring group in front of Wooden Horse

Troy was a city in northwest Anatolia, but best known as the setting of the Trojan War described in the Greek Epic Cycle (and especially in *The Iliad*, one of two epic poems attributed to Homer). A new city called Ilium was founded on the site during the reign of Roman Emperor Augustus. It flourished until the establishment of Constantinople and gradually declined during the Byzantine era.

The region's history goes way back 3,000 years, when the Trojan War was waged against the city of Troy by the Achaeans after a prince of Troy took Helen from her husband Menelaus, king of Sparta. *The Iliad* describes part of the last year of the siege of Troy, and *The Odyssey* describes Odysseus' journey home.

I watched the movie version of the Trojan War and read a translation of *The Iliad*, in which the Achaeans set up camp near the mouth of the River Scamander and anchored their ships. The city of Troy stood on a hill, across the plain of Scamander, where the battles of the Trojan War took place. The site of the ancient city is some three miles from the coast today, but the river poured into a large bay that formed a natural harbor 3,000 years ago. It has since been filled with alluvial material. Recent geological findings have permitted the reconstruction of the original Trojan coastline, and the results largely confirm the accuracy of the Troy's of Homer.

Besides *The Iliad*, there are references to Troy in *The Odyssey* and other Greek literature. The Homeric legend of Troy was elaborated on by the Roman poet Virgil in his *Aeneid*. The Greeks and Romans took the Trojan War and the existence of Troy as historical fact. Alexander the Great, for example, visited the site in 334 B.C. and made sacrifices at tombs associated with Achilles and Patroclus.

With the rise of modern history, Troy and the Trojan War were consigned to the realms of legend. However, the exact location of ancient Troy had always been a subject of speculation, until 1822, when Scottish journalist Charles Maclaren identified the location of the acropolis of Augustus' New Ilium in north-western Anatolia.

Ephesus

Ephesus was an ancient Greek city, then, a major Roman city, and is now a Turkish city on the west coast of Asia Minor. In the first century B.C., it had a population of some 250,000, making it one of the largest cities in the Mediterranean world.

Ephesus also was one of the seven churches of Asia, cited in the biblical book of Revelation. The Gospel of John may also have been written there. The city was the site of several fifth century Christian councils. The house where the Virgin Mary spent her last days and where she died in the presence of Saint John was near Ephesus.

Celsus Library

    We took a guided tour of Ephesus, the site of the largest collection of Roman ruins in the eastern Mediterranean—and only 15% has been excavated. The ruins that are visible give some idea of the city's original splendor, and the names associated with the ruins are evocative of its former glory. A theater dominates the view down Harbor Street, which leads to the ancient harbor. The Celsus Library stands tall, reflecting the ancient grandeur of Ephesus, as shown on the back of Turkish 20 TL bill.

Koreans tourists visit the area as a Christian holy place with an easy access from the port of Kusadasi. I met a few young Korean couples with their school-age children in a Korean restaurant and asked how they could take a vacation during the middle of May. They all seemed surprised and told me that touring Ephesus was more important for their children than school works. I had never considered taking a vacation with our children when school was in session, but I had to nod my head to show that I agreed with them.

Turkish style Korean food with its fresh red peppers and hot sauce wasn't my favorite, but it was much better than the Greek or Turkish dishes we had been eating on our tour.

I was amazed to see baths of Varius and Scholastikia, built in the firt century. Scholastikia baths had four rooms: cold, lukewarm, hot, and sweating just like Roman baths, and the whole interiors were laid with natural marbles. There also were dressing room, resting room, a library and a gymnasium. The bath could serve a thousand people.

Mr. Kim, our tour guide had come to Turkey about thirteen years earlier to study the art history of the region. He worked part-time as a tour guide, but his main job was collecting and selling arts. His revelations and emotional interpretations of the historical site were excellent.

Saint John came to Ephesus in 42 A.D. with the Virgin Mary and lived and died in the city after spreading the message of Christianity. Saint Paul, who came to the city in 52 A.D, formed a Christian society and stayed there for three years. Some Christians among our group were touched when they stood in front of the Saint John tomb, and prayed.

A church with a wooden roof was built on the site in the fourth century with a monument indicating the location of Saint John's grave. Emperor Justinian, later, built a basilica with the tomb of Saint John tomb beneath a dome in the middle.

After walking many miles around the ancient city, we drove to Kuşadasi, a resort town on Turkey's Aegean coast and a center of art and culture since the founding Leleges people in 3,000 B.C. Later settlers included the Aeolians in the eleventh century B.C. and the Ionians in the ninth century B.C. From the window of our luxurious hotel, we had a glorious view of the Kusadasi harbor.

Pamukkale and Hierapolis

Pamukkale [cotton castle] in Turkey's Inner Aegean region is a site of natural hot springs and travertine, terraces of carbonate minerals left by the flowing water.

The ancient Greco-Roman and Byzantine city of Hierapolis was built on top of the white "castle," which is about 8,860 ft. long, 1,970 ft. wide, and 525 ft. high. It can be seen from the hills on the opposite side of the valley in the town of Denizli. This huge city was built to be used as a resort for kings, queens, generals and dignitaries.

Our tour guide added a personal side as we viewed the site, "I'm so glad I wasn't born in those days," because more than 10,000 slaves and other poor citizens were exploited during the building of the magnificent city.

People have bathed in its pools for thousands of years, but as recently as the mid-twentieth century hotels were being built over the ruins of Hierapolis, causing considerable damage to the ancient site. An approach road was built from the valley over the terraces and motor bikes were allowed to go up and down the slopes. When the area was declared a World Heritage site, the hotels were demolished and the road removed.

We checked into a hotel under the "castle" and enjoyed swimming in modern hot spring pools, which had Turkish massage facilities. The ladies in our group were tempted to indulge in expensive cosmetic massages. I asked if they had a Japanese version of a "Turkish bath for men," imported by American soldiers in 1945. They had no idea I was talking about a steam bath, followed by a massage given by nearly naked woman.

In the museum, alongside historical artifacts from Hierapolis, there were artifacts from Laodiceia, Colossae, Tripolis, Attuda, and other towns of the Lycos valley. The artifacts in open exhibition space are mostly made of marble and stone. The museum's exhibition space consisted of three closed areas of the Hierapolis bath and open areas on the eastern side, which was known to have been used as a library and gymnasium.

The underground volcanic activity that causes the hot springs also forces carbon dioxide into a cave, which was called the Plutonium (home of the god Pluto). The cave was used for religious purposes by priests of Cybele, who were apparently immune to the suffocating gas.

Cappadocia

Cappadocia is a historical region in Central Anatolia. The Cappadocians were believed to occupy the whole region, from Mount Taurus to the vicinity of the Black Sea.

We were overwhelmed by the natural wonders of the underground cities, which were used by early Christians as hiding places before Christianity became an accepted religion.

The underground cities included vast defense networks spread throughout many levels. Those defenses were very creative, including large round stones to block doors and holes in ceilings through which defenders could drop spears. The tunnel system consisted of thin corridors that made it impossible for groups of Romans to move in.

Bosphorus Bridge

Istanbul

Istanbul, formerly called Constantinople, is Turkey's largest city, with a population of 13.4 millions, and lies on the Bosphorus Strait, extending onto the European and Asian sides. Istanbul is the only city in the world situated on two continents.

During its long history, Istanbul has served as the capital of the Roman Empire, the Byzantine Empire, the Latin Empire, and the Ottoman Empire. When the Republic of Turkey was established in 1923, Ankara was chosen as its capital.

Constantinople began to decline after the Fourth Crusade, during which it was sacked and pillaged. The city subsequently became the center of the Latin Empire, created by Catholic crusaders to replace the Orthodox Byzantine Empire, which had divided into splinter states. However, the Latin Empire was short-lived, and the Byzantine Empire was restored, in 1261. Constantinople's churches, defenses, and basic services were in disrepair, and its population had dwindled to 40,000 from nearly half a million in the ninth century.

Eastside Bosphorus Strait and Blue Mosque

Following the fall of Constantinople, Mehmed II immediately set out to revitalize the city, now known as Istanbul. First he deported all the Christian population, leaving only the Jewish inhabitants of Balat. Then he forcibly resettled many Muslims, Jews, and Christians from other parts of Anatolia and Rumelia into the city, creating a cosmopolitan society that persisted throughout much of the Ottoman period.

Istanbul's strategic position along the historic Silk Road, rail networks to Europe and the Middle East, and the only sea route between the Black Sea and the Mediterranean have helped foster an eclectic populace, although less so since the establishment of Turkish Republic.

Overlooked for the new capital during much of the twentieth century, the city has regained much of its prominence. The city's population has increased tenfold since the 1950s, as migrants from across Anatolia flocked to the metropolis.

Commuter ferries have been operating on the Bosphorus since 1851 and are the primary mode of public transportation between the European and Asian halves of the city. We toured the Bosphorus Strait and the beautiful city of Istanbul by a boat.

Hagia Sophia is a former Orthodox basilica which later was converted into a mosque, and is now a museum in Istanbul. The church was dedicated to the *Logos,* of the Holy Trinity. Although it's sometimes referred to as the Church of Saint Sophia, *sophia* is a phonetic Latin spelling of the Greek word for wisdom.

Famous for its massive dome, it's considered the epitome of Byzantine architecture, and is said to have "changed the history of architecture." It was the largest cathedral in the world for nearly a thousand years, until Spain's Seville Cathedral was completed in 1520.

In 1453, Constantinople was conquered by the Ottoman Turks, who ordered the building converted into a mosque. The bells, altar, and sacrificial vessels were removed and many of the church's mosaics were plastered over. Four minarets were added, and the building remained a mosque until 1931. It was closed to the public for four years and then re-opened as a museum in 1935.

Topkapi Palace

    The Topkapi Palace was the primary residence of the Ottoman sultans for approximately 400 years of their 624-year reign. As well as a royal residence, the palace was the setting for state occasions and royal entertainments. It's now a major tourist attraction containing important holy relics of the Muslim world, including the Prophet Muhammad's cloak and sword.

    The palace complex consists of four main courtyards and many smaller buildings. At its peak, the palace was home to as many as 4,000 people. The complex was expanded over the centuries to contain mosques, a hospital, bakeries, and a mint. The name translates as "Cannon Gate Palace," referring to a nearby gate that was long ago destroyed.

    The Topkapi Palace gradually lost importance as sultans began to spend more time in their new palaces along the Bosporus. With the end of the Ottoman Empire in 1921, the palace was transformed into a museum of the Imperial era. The palace complex has hundreds of rooms, but only the most important are accessible to the public. The museum includes large collections of porcelain, robes, weapons, shields, and armor as well as a display of Ottoman treasures and jewelry.

    Our tour plan of Istanbul included shopping, and we were escorted through the grand bazaar in Istanbul, which is the oldest and largest shopping center of the world with its sixty-four streets and roads, two covered bazaars, sixteen inns, and about 3,600 shops. Our guide emphasized that all prices in the various shops were negotiable—sometimes down to as much as 50% of the original asking price. The complex looked just like the old South Gate Market in Seoul, although prices aren't negotiable.

C. LAOS

A Country of Communism and Buddhism

\Laos is one of the world's few remaining Communist states and I wished to see this Buddhist country to compare with North Korea and Nicaragua in South America. The Pha That Luang (Great Stupa) is a gold-covered large Buddhist stupa in the center of Vientiane, Laos. It is generally regarded as the most important national monument and national symbol.

Exploring Laos was planned as one of two travel plans of 2019, after cruising the Antarctic and South America in March. Laos is a landlocked nation surrounded by Vietnam, China, Myanmar, Thailand and Cambodia and is the last country for us to see on the Indochina peninsula.

Laos became a Communist country in 1975 following a revolution supported by Vietnam and the Soviet Union. The country's government is largely run by military generals who support a one-party communist system. Since 1988, the country, however, began allowing some forms of private ownership and foreign tourists and investments.

When we landed in a Vientiane International Airport around midnight of September 24, 2019 and drove to a newly built tourist hotel, we did not see traffic signal lights or policemen on main streets of the capital city. We found lots of motor cycles and cars on the streets, but no major traffic jam as we had seen in Bangkok or Ho Chi Min City.

Laos has a population of about 7 million living on a large 92 thousand square miles. Estimated their per capita income is about 3,000 dollars. In this communist country, there are super rich people in Vientiane, while poor farmers live in rural areas, where dogs, cows and pigs are on highways and residential areas. I was wondering how they find their animals.

Most of the streets of rural towns are not paved and covered with yellow dust from rich soil. While rich people in Vientiane live in modern houses, the living conditions of farmers in rural towns seem to be very poor. In contradiction, the overall happiness index is higher than any other developed countries such as Japan or South Korea, according to our tour guide.

During our journey of three days, we did not meet any policeman or soldiers, but our tour guide told us that the ruling Communist Party has a strong power to control people, and their moving to urban cities was strictly controlled just like in North Korea.

Historically, Laos was established as Lan Xang Hom Khao (1354–1707), which existed for four centuries as one of the largest kingdoms in Southeast Asia. Due to Lan Xang's central geographical location in Southeast Asia, the kingdom became a popular hub for overland trade, becoming wealthy economically as well as culturally.

In 1893, Laos became a French protectorate. It briefly gained independence in 1945 after the Japanese occupation, but was recolonized by France until Laos became an independent country in 1953, with a constitutional monarchy. Shortly after independence, a long civil war began, which saw the Communist resistance, supported by the Soviet Union, fight against, first, the monarchy and then a number of military dictatorships, supported by the United States.

After the Vietnam War ended in 1975, the Communist Pathet Lao movement came to power, ending the civil war. During the first years of Communist rule, Laos was dependent on military and economic aid by the Soviet Union, until the dissolution of the Soviet Union in 1991.

Laos is a multi-ethnic country, with the politically and culturally dominant Lao people make up about 55 percent of the population, mostly in the lowlands. Mon-Khmer groups, the Hmong, and other indigenous hill tribes, accounting for 45 percent of the population, live in the foothills and mountains.

Unlike the strong French influence in Vietnam, we did not find any sign of French culture and Catholicism. Our tour guide told us there was 1 percent Christian in the country, when I asked him, and we did not see any Christian church.

Buddhism in Laos

Religion in general is not supported by communist countries. But the single ruling communist party in Laos uses Buddhism for their political purposes to control any movement to protest their dictatorial political structure and policies.

Buddhism is the world's fourth-largest religion with over 520 million followers, or over 7% of the global population, known as Buddhists. Buddhism encompasses a variety of traditions, beliefs and spiritual practices largely based on original teachings attributed to the Buddha and resulting interpreted philosophies. Buddhism originated in ancient India as a Sramana tradition sometime between the 6th and 4th centuries BC, spreading through much of Asia.

Most Buddhist traditions share the goal of overcoming suffering and the cycle of death and rebirth, either by the attainment of Nirvana or through the path of Buddhahood.

Buddhist schools vary in their interpretation of the path to liberation, the relative importance and canonicity assigned to the various Buddhist texts, and their specific teachings and practices. Widely observed practices include taking refuge in the Buddha, the Dharma and the Sangha, observance of moral precepts, monasticism, meditation, and the cultivation of the Paramitas (virtues).

Buddhists in this Communist country count for 64,7% and Tai folk religion that also is very similar to Buddhism for 31.4%. The dominant 96.1 % of the population of this religion. is well respected by the ruling Communist government.

And the Buddhist Sangha in Laos, therefore, has expanded their traditional role of teaching Buddhism to assisting in adult literacy programs. They teach the Lao language and other subjects in places where schools are not available or where teachers are not available.

They play a prominent role in education, especially early education. They continue their role as traditional healers in a country where doctors are scarce. The Sangha is now seen as a preserver of national culture, especially in the maintenance of wats and monasteries.

Buddhism is often closely tied to animist beliefs and belief in ancestral spirits, particularly in rural areas.

Buddhists in Laos are very devout, and in the past almost every Lao man joined a monastery, or temple, for at least a short period of time. Some men also become monks for the rest of their lives. Because of the demands of modern life, this practice is currently undergoing changes. Most people donate money to the monks to gain merit and improve their Karma. Lao monks are highly respected and revered in Lao communities.

Based on Laotian Buddhism, according to our guide, the women of Laos are taught that they can only attain nirvana after they have been reborn as men.

On the first day of our tour, we went to Patuxai which means "Victory Gate." It was built during a turbulent period in Lao history, when Laos was a constitutional monarchy. It was dedicated to the memory of the Laotian soldiers who died during World War II and the war for independence from France in 1949.

The monument was built using American funds and cement actually intended to build a new airport. The Royal Laotian Government instead built the monument.

In May 1975, the Communist Pathet Lao overthrew the coalition government and seized power, ending the ancient monarchy and installing a half-Vietnamese prime minister. They renamed the monument Patuxai in honor of the victory that was handed to them by the North Vietnamese Army.

Interior rooms were decorated with depictions of the gods Vishnu, Brahma, and Indra from left to right. The monument has five towers that represent the five principles of coexistence among nations of the world.

They are also representative of the five Buddhist principles of "thoughtful amiability, flexibility, honesty, honor and prosperity." I was surprised to find small shopping tables filled the five story rooms of the national monument.

Wat Si Muang is one of Vientiane's most popular sites of worship, and offers a fascinating insight into how old animist beliefs have blended seamlessly with Theravada Buddhism.

According to local legend, when the temple was being built in 1563 a young pregnant woman named Si Muang volunteered to sacrifice herself to appease the angry spirits. She threw herself into a hole in the ground where the building's central pillar was to be placed, and was crushed when the massive pillar was lowered into position. This central pillar also formed the center of the town that was springing up around Wat Si Muang, which to this day is revered as the 'mother temple' of Vientiane.

During our tour of this Buddhist temple, we observed a ceremony of blessing for a newly bought car by monk. Our tour guide told us that many Laotians bring their new cell phones, television set or any furniture to this temple for a monk's blessing.

During the That Luang Festival every October or November, this temple is one of the focal points of the celebrations, and Si Muang is celebrated as a guardian of the city. On a daily basis, Wat Si Muang attracts crowds of local Buddhists who want to benefit from its 'good luck' powers. It is commonly thought that if you pray for something here and simultaneously make a promise, your wish will be granted, providing you return and fulfil your promise.

King Sisavang Vong's monument is located next door, and is reachable through a gate from the Wat Si Muang grounds.

The Vientiane Night Market is a quieter and cleaner version of other tourist markets found in South East Asia.

The Vientiane Night market, however, also has a lot in common with other night markets in Asia. The items for sale are consistent with what you find throughout region: inexpensive clothes and souvenirs take up most of the stalls, including T-shirts, local crafts, electronic gadgets, phone covers and underwear.

What's missing from this particular market are the counterfeit DVDs and food stalls. Set on a promenade in front of the Mekong River, this is a great place to stroll around before the sun sets. Shopping or browsing can be combined with eating out in restaurants, going to the park, or watching the sun set over the Mekong.

In true Lao style, the market is very laid back. The sellers are not very pushy and leave you alone to browse their stalls. Foreigners are also more likely to find clothes that fit here than other markets in Vientiane.

Hmong Conflict

Some Hmong groups fought as CIA-backed units on the Royalist side in the Laotian Civil War. After the Pathet Lao took over the country in 1975, the conflict continued in isolated pockets. In 1977, a Communist newspaper promised the party would hunt down the "American collaborators" and their families "to the last root".

As many as 200,000 Hmong went into exile in Thailand, with many ending up in the US. A number of Hmong fighters hid out in the mountains in for many years, with a remnant emerging from the jungle in 2003.

In 1989, the United Nations High Commissioner for Refugees (UNHCR), with the support of the US government, instituted the Comprehensive Plan of Action, a program to stem the tide of Indochinese refugees from Laos, Vietnam, and Cambodia. Under the plan, refugee status was evaluated through a screening process. Recognized asylum seekers were given resettlement opportunities, while the remaining refugees were to be repatriated under guarantee of safety.

After completing our planned tour around Vientiane, we drove our van-north up to a stretch of high mountains to reach Vang Vieng, which was, according to our tour guide, first settled around 1353 as a staging post between Luang Prabang and Vientiane.

Vang Vieng was used by American troops during the 1964-73 Vietnam War by constructing an air force base and runway. The airstrip was then called "Lima site 6". In more recent times, the town has grown substantially due to the influx of tourists attracted by the opportunities for adventure activities in the limestone Karst mountains and Nam Song River.

Attractions of the town include inner tubing and kayaking on the Nam Song River, which was equipped with rope swings, zip lines, swimming and diving into a blue lagoon, and large decks for socializing. Other activities include trekking and rock climbing in the limestone mountains. There are also numerous caves.

Due to the influx of backpackers, according to our guide, Vang Vieng locals have seen drastic changes in their community. In recent years, Vang Vieng has become a stop on the Southeast Asia backpacker circuit and the main street has many guest houses, bars, restaurants, internet cafes and tour agencies.

Residents in this new tourist town are concerned that the town is in danger of losing its charm as it becomes full of tourists, mushroom shakes, and many bars. Floating on tubes combined with heavy drinking has resulted in many tourist drownings.

We rented a dune buggy for two hours and raced to go to the blue lagoons of Vang Vieng on four wheels. We were given heavy sunglasses and a bandana for the dusty dirt roads and cruised around in style.

We also swam in the Blue Lagoon

Vang Vieng, we were told by our guide, had three blue lagoons that were accessible as part of a packaged tour, including visiting caves, swimming in the lagoons, hiking and tubing. We did not miss any opportunity to explore these beautiful natural wonders.

Zip Lining

Our package included zip lining at a Blue Lagoon and back and forth over the Nam Song. We also explored on a tire tube around the inside of a cave, Tham Lom Cave, near the zip lining area. We could see the picturesque formation of the cave by wearing a helmet with mining head lamp.

We also took a kayak, which was maneuvered by a professional and floated with the current down the Nam Song. Our boat picked up the pace on the rapids of the nearby Nam Ngum, and we took in the rice paddies and mountains on the west bank, and waved at the tourists in town on the east bank.

We are experienced canoers on the Current River, which flows into Arkansas and Missouri. During our living in Missouri for 30 years, we took advantage of exploring the Current, that is spring-fed, giving it a somewhat constant water flow throughout the year. The Current River was our favorite river for fishing smallmouth bass and canoeing. But the river flows on a flat land unlike the Nam Song. We were amazed to see high limestone mountains along the Nam Song river.

The Nam Song River is a small river in Laos that flows through the town of Vang Vieng. It is a popular tourist destination as many people enjoy seeing the Laotian countryside while going down the river in a kayak. The river is surrounded by striking karst rock formations. Upstream from Vang Vieng, numerous bars have been built on the river's banks to attract the tourists floating by.

On our way back to Korea in a plane, Boeing 737-800, I wondered about the official name of country, "Lao People's Democratic Republic." Most of Communist countries use the word of democracy, while the United States of America or Republic of Korea do not use the word in the names of their countries.

I looked up a definition of democracy in Webster dictionary. It said "a: government by the people; especially: rule of the majority. b: a government in which the supreme power is vested in the people and exercised by them directly or indirectly through a system of representation usually involving periodically held free elections."

During my visits to these three countries, I found out that Communist countries also use election, but most of their votes are cast to approve or disapprove the candidates or policies, which were chosen by the ruling parties, and most of their elections were approved by over 95 percent. Their elections are a form of democracy used to disguise for their dictatorial functions.

Socialism is a good ideology, which has not found a way to achieve the goal of "equality" and to improve the quality of living of all the people. It has been good for the ruling Communist party, and makes people equal by being all poor without any incentive for working hard.

I also discovered that there was no big private company to compete with the big corporations of the developed countries which are in fierce competition for world trade, and that their economic situation had gotten worse since their "revolution." GNP per capita of these three countries was better than South Korea in the early 1970s. Now these Communist countries are far behind, ten to twenty times from South Korea.

When I arrived back in Seoul, I was told that the current President and his ruling political party have been trying to work toward a socialistic country and to coexist with North Korea in order to avoid any war between Koreans. I firmly believe that their goal is a dream that would not work for South Korea.

D. Hong Kong

Hong Kong

When we arrived in Hong Kong in September 2010, we were amazed at the ultramodern airport, high-rise buildings, and well dressed, energetic people. It had been only 13 years, since I had been here when the "perfume harbor" had been transferred to China. I had been impressed with Seoul folks, but the changes in Hong Kong seemed even more fantastic.

Hong Kong was the only gate to China in the early years following the pulling back of the Bamboo Curtain of Red China. Our first visit was in 1984, when Young and I were invited to Taiwan as special guests of then Chairman of the Central News Agency, S.Y. Ma. It had been arranged for us to tour Macau and the birthplace of Sun Yat-sen in the southern part of China via Hong Kong. We visited again on our way to Beijing in 1986, where we also toured Xian, Shanghai, and Yanbian.

The most memorable visit for us to the densely populated city, however, was in 1997, when the British Empire turned Hong Kong over to China. I had been invited to write a report of the ceremony for the *Munhwa Daily News* in Korea. I predicted that the international harbor would be the main gate for bringing in the hidden capital of the so-called Overseas Chinese in southwestern countries, where many Chinese businessmen had been successful and were looking for safe ways to invest their hidden capital.

I also predicted that the Chinese government wouldn't change the administrative function of the city, since they needed it to be prosperous, even though many Chinese people, fearing the changeover, had moved to Richmond, British Columbia, a suburb of Vancouver, where they established "Hongcouver." Many Chinese-Canadian businessmen later returned to Hong Kong to run their businesses while leaving their families in the relative safety of Canada.

We went to Hong Kong for nine days to visit our son, Anthony now grown with a family of his own and working in Hong Kong as a Senior Counsel for the Philip Morris International Corporation. Anthony took a week's vacation to show us around a truly international gem of a city.

Anthony told us a number of amazing stories as he drove us to his apartment on Hong Kong Island, and he was especially intrigued by how much the Chinese folks love the number *eight*, which sounds similar to the words "prosper" or "wealth" in the Chinese language. Because of its supposed significance, folks in Hong Kong and China pay extra money to have eights in their phone numbers, street addresses, driver's license numbers, and bank account numbers.

One vehicle license plate with eights was auctioned for more than a million Chinese dollars (about $150,000) and a telephone number comprised of all eights sold for a quarter of a million U.S. dollars. The opening ceremony of the Bank of China in Hong Kong was held at 8:00 on August 8, 1988, and the Beijing Olympics began on August 8, 2008 at 8 minutes and 8 seconds past 8 p.m.

The value of eight could also be linked to Buddhism and the meaning of the lotus flower with eight petals. An ingenious system was adopted by the developers of 39 Conduit Road in Hong Kong, where the top floor was called "88," offering future residents double fortune.

On the other hand, it's common in Hong Kong for the fourth floor of buildings not to exist. In fact, in that same 39 Conduit Road development, forty-three floor numbers are omitted, including 14, 24, 34, 64, and all the floors between 40 and 59. The floor number following 68 is 88.

Hong Kong residents live in either the most expensive housing or the least expensive, such as boat houses. However, they don't seem to cook much at home. Instead, rich and poor can be found in the many fine restaurants, such as the five-story floating Jumbo restaurant. It was disconcerting to see a boat in the center of the surrounding high-rise apartments.

When we went to Taikooshing, a giant shopping mall where we needed to pick up our grandson, Alex from the Delia School of Canada, we were amazed by the signs of affluence not present in many American malls. Shopping isn't my favorite way to spend holiday time, but Young enjoyed it. We were delighted to meet our first granddaughter (who was six months old at that time), but she wasn't so happy about meeting strangers at first. Alex was in second grade and promised me he'd eventually go to Harvard.

Anthony's apartment was on South Bay Road on Repulse Bay, and from the twentieth floor, I felt like I was on a high-rise cruise boat, looking down at the water through the all-glass walls. The rent on his gorgeous apartment was an incredible $15,000 a month, which amounts to about $500 a day. As a professor at a state university, I had never stayed in any hotel that expensive and continue to shop around for a less expensive motel as a retiree, but I enjoyed the luxury.

Young people generally tend to be better off than the preceding generation, because as society accumulates knowledge, the youth of the world translate it into wealth. For more than 100 years, from the time of Karl Marx until the latter part of the twentieth century, economists looked at capital accumulation as the main factor in economic growth. Under Marxist economics, the capitalists accumulate wealth while workers remain miserable until they finally get fed up and launch a revolution. The idea that saving leads to wealth isn't wrong, but saving isn't the only road to wealth—for a nation or an individual. In fact, most people living under communist dictatorships are worse off than ordinary workers under capitalism.

Two hundred years ago, when labor efficiency was growing slowly, inherited wealth or the lack thereof played an important role in determining a person's social station. With the acceleration of technological change, inherited capital matters less and personal earning power and savings matter more. The growth of your personal "efficiency of labor" will be a big factor in determining your future social status. If you make good use of your education and enthusiastically adapt to take advantage of technological advances over the next thirty years, you'll get rich. If you don't, you'll gradually slip to a lower status.

I've heard many complaints from my friends about the attitudes of today's young people, especially when we meet young ladies playing golf on exclusive courses during working hours. Our wives never would have dreamed of spending money so frivolously when they were young, but the world has definitely changed.

Another luxury in Hong Kong is to own and drive a car on the narrow roads, especially when gasoline costs more than $7.00 a gallon. Anthony told us that he had to pay half the price of his expensive Mercedes sedan to the government just to get his license plate. He also had a special pass card that clicked every time he approached a bridge, tunnel, or even a parking lot.

On Monday evening, when Hong Kong sky was clear for the first time since we had arrived, we were treated to a fantastic view of Hong Kong's night sky from the Philip Morris International yacht. We cruised around the harbor and then visited Kui Kee seafood restaurant on Hoi Pang Road, where we feasted on lobster, bamboo oyster, scallops, shrimp, scorpions, and perch. The food was very good and reasonably priced.

Anthony used most of the services of the Aberdeen Marina Club, a private club where members and their families enjoy superb facilities of more than 550,000 square feet with six restaurants, a swimming pool, boat docks, and plenty of parking spaces. Club membership costs around $300,000. Anthony invited Brian Bogard and his wife to the club with us. The Bogards had just moved to Hong Kong to work for PMI, the same company Anthony works for. I've known Brian since his high school days.

When we visited Lantau Island, we asked Alex's schoolmates to join us. The landscape of the island had recently been transformed by the development of several major projects, including the new Hong Kong International Airport, the Ngong Ping 360 cable car, and Hong Kong Disneyland.

Lantau, the former site of a fishing village, is the largest island in Hong Kong, located at the mouth of the Pearl River, and contains several national parks with campsites and youth hostels. Lantau's best-known and longest beach is Cheung Sha, and its most famous hike is to Sunset Peak, the third highest elevation in Hong Kong.

Ngong Ping 360 combines a 5.7 km cable car journey with a cultural-themed village and easy access to the Tian Tan Buddha statue, the world's largest (eighty-five feet tall) outdoor bronze statue of a seated Buddha. The cable car travels between Tung Chung and Ngong Ping terminals and provided a spectacular twenty-five-minute experience with panoramic views of the statue, the flora and fauna of North Lantau Park, Tung Chung Bay, and the airport.

We also visited Po Lin monastery is a Zen temple, founded in 1906 by three monks visiting from China and which was initially known as "The Big Hut." It was renamed in 1924. It's ironic that those monks chose that remote mountain for their monastery. Zen monks have few personal possessions and sometimes cut off all relations with the outside world. A hermit-recluse lifestyle is considered of paramount importance. Over the years, the commercially enterprising government has turned that sacred place into a public playground with many tourist shops.

Another tradition in Asia is to ask a stone or bronze Buddha for help with personal problems. Many people walked up to the Tian Tan Buddha to request help for their children in passing college entrance exams or to cure the health problems of family members. I'm not sure if such practice is written about in Buddhist literature, but it's common in Asia.

To me, the best tourist spot in Hong Kong is called The Eagle's Peak, where we chose to spend a day. Driving a car from Repulse Bay to The Peak during morning rush hour was quite an experience, but at least the traffic moved slowly, as opposed to "not moving" in other areas like Bangkok or Seoul.

I had visited The Peak many years earlier, when there was much less development, especially hotels and apartments. Right under The Peak and Hong Kong Park, a huge Pacific Shopping Plaza and Shangri-La Hotel had been built, including a convenient but expensive underground parking lot. Hong Kong Park was officially opened in May 1991. The site was originally a garrison named Victoria Barracks. In 1979, the government decided that the portion of the garrison near the foot of the hill would be used for commercial development and construction of government buildings while the mid-level portion would be jointly developed by the Urban Council and the Royal Hong Kong Jockey Club for the provision of a park.

The Peak Tower is one of the most stylish architectural icons in Hong Kong. With an avant-garde design representing the epitome of modern architecture, the spectacular tower has been featured in millions of photographs and postcards. The Peak Tower also features a dazzling array of restaurants, shops, and entertainment venues, all set against the beautiful backdrop of the city. The tower also provides Hong Kong's highest 360° viewing platform, the Sky Terrace, which offers a spectacular panoramic view.

We also wanted to see in a local market like the South Gate Market in Seoul, and I was delighted to find Stanley Market near Repulse Bay. Stanley was a sleepy fishing village before British settlement, but it has grown to become a modern city with plenty of excellent places to eat, good beaches, and a large market to shop for clothes, silk, and souvenirs.

A notable place in Stanley was the old police station, which was built during the late nineteenth century but is now home to many restaurants. The Japanese used the building as a headquarters during World War II. We had lunch in Mijas, which was well decorated inside and out and served a fancy menu. My classic martini with lunch was superb and reasonably priced.

Cruising on the top of Philip Morris International yacht.

4. 80th Birthday Celebration

祝八旬 장원호 김영숙

Happy 80th Birthday

김영숙 여사
장원호 박사
祝八旬宴

2016 was a very special year for us. Our three children and their spouses planned a big family party in celebration of our 80th birthdays in the Korean tradition. Koreans count one year ahead to when the baby was conceived.

The party plan was initiated in November, 2015, when I went to Seoul to receive a Distinguished Service Award by the Missouri Alumni Association in Korea. May 28th was chosen to be able to reserve the big dining hall of the Seoul Club and to accommodate vacation times for Susan and Eugene's families.

The exclusive Seoul Club's main dining hall is elegant and in a convenient location next to the Shilla Hotel. Due to the limited size, we could not invite my 200 former students who were living in Korea.

We decided instead to limit the party to family members. I have four living brothers and three sisters, and Young has three brothers and two sisters without counting her first younger brother James, who died two years ago.

From our 15 siblings, there are over 50 children, grandchildren and one great grandchild. We also invited some friends. Young's brothers and sisters with their children from Daegu rented a large tourist bus to come to Seoul, and Prisca, Young's younger sister with her two daughters, Helen and Cecilia, came from Canada.

The program was organized by Damee and Chihyung, and the master of ceremonies was Dr. Chulho, our nephew and professor of Yonsei University Medical School. Our three children paid for the expenses. We followed their instructions as arranged.

祝八旬宴 김영숙 여사
장원호 박사

Flowers from Tobin and Chloe

We were dressed in Korean traditional costume, and escorted to the party. Many guests had already arrived before us. We were seated at the head table that was gracefully decorated with flowers and a placard which said "Happy 80th Birthday for Dr. Won Ho Chang and Mrs. Young Sook Kim," in Korean.

Once everyone has arrived, Dr. Chulho opened the ceremony with his brief introduction, followed by Anthony's introduction of family members, and I greeted distinguished guests.

As planned, Tobin and Chloe came to the head table with flowers for us as the initiation of the ceremony. Damee and Chihyung helped the kids during this procedure.

Eric and Ben   Susan and David

Damee and Chloe   Alex and Anthony

Tessa, Tobin & Eugene

The second part of the program was our children's greetings: First, Susan's family came to the head table and in the traditional manner, poured two cups of Korean rice wine, handed the cups to us, and bowed. Next Anthony and Eugene's family also followed the ritual.

The third part was singing the birthday song by guests accompanied by Alex on violin and Damee on piano.

The birthday toast was led by Yang, Hwee Boo, the Commissioner of the Korean Professional Golf Association and my former student.

The first congratulatory remark was made by Dr. Jang Han Rhee, chairman of Chong-Geun-Dang Pharmaceutical Group. He wished us a very happy birthday. Dr. Rhee asked us to invite him to the next future centennial birthday party.

Then, Dr. Daichul Chyung, a former presidential candidate of the country followed with his prepared remarks. Dr. Chyung is a leading politician in Korea who received his doctoral degree in political science from the University of Missouri in the 1970s. We have been close friends since Young and his wife bought and operated a laundry shop in 1972. This was when I had started my teaching and Daichul had started his graduate program.

Dr. Chyung said that he liked me for the following four reasons: 1) "Professor Chang" has a strong sense of balance and acts on the basis of his reasoning. He was repeatedly asked to be part of Korean politics, but he stayed with teaching to great success. I personally respect his decision and actions. 2) He takes a very humble attitude toward his contribution of educating journalists and helping Korean scholars. He has trained more than 200 Korean journalists and 19 schol-

Dr. DC Chyung

Juah and Dr. Rhee

ars. He rarely brags about his achievements and students. He does not call them when he comes to Korea as he is afraid of burdening his former students.

3) He is so kind and friendly that I feel as if I'm meeting my own brother. He treats all his former students in this manner. 4) Finally, I cannot forget about our laundry business partner with whom I have so many nostalgic memories. I like him, and wish him and his wife a healthy and happy 20 plus years, so that I can also attend their future centennial celebration.

The Kims Families

Young and I responded that we were deeply honored by this celebration. We were especially grateful for the work of Damee and Chihyung to make this party so successful. We also expressed our thanks to distinguished guests and family members who joined us for this great event.

Food was served, and we mingled to exchange endless stories about anything or everything.

After 86 years

After 86 years, I've realized the simple truth that my family and friends are an integral part of my happiness.

I also discovered my joy in life when working hard to overcome the challenges and adversity caused by unforeseen events, destiny, or divine providence. I had worked hard to overcome the difficulties of being a poor international student. I had achieved my goal of receiving three degrees: BA, MA and Ph.D. in six years in the United States. After receiving three degrees, I had worked hard to support the education of my three children, while I had been devoted to helping hundreds of students in their journalism careers.

After my retirement, I have been working full time traveling, reading, writing and publishing books. I wrote a book in Korean in 2007 called "Retirement without Retiring," which explains the components and ideal types of retirement.   The book also concludes that retirement can require more than a full time job. I am busier now than before the retirement. When I have any spare time, I travel around the world with a particular fondness for the beautiful mountains and Buddhist temples in my beloved country, Korea.

I worked hard to establish a system to publish books through amazon.com, which is selling my eight books and two other books, authored by others. In 2014 I also created the Korean Book Club (KBC) in Laguna Woods Village to help members publish their autobiographies.

I even enjoy working on projects like home improvement and exotic cooking. As a part of my retirement, I enjoy tending a garden that is thriving with vegetables and citrus fruits. I enjoy working.

I believe the remainder of my life should be devoted to the happiness of others instead of my own. I am devoting my work to my wife of 55 years, my three children, their spouses, and five grandchildren.

I also believe my physical fitness needs to be a vital part of my retirement agenda. Playing golf had been my major exercise before reaching my age of 85 years. Golfing takes too many hours of my valuable time, and I hate to make so many mistakes hitting the golf ball. I found other types of exercise fit my current needs.

Walking is at the top of my list. I walk around my neighborhood as much as I have the opportunity. Walking helps me move my body while I enjoy meditating, looking at flowers, trees and blue sky, while singing my old nostalgic songs. I also include my old exercises of swimming and weight lifting.

I used to enjoy watching sports, like football, baseball, basketball and golf. I rarely watch television these days. The thrilling excitement and suspension of the games, news and entertainment disturb my peace of mind. I'd rather read the books of philosophers like Goethe, Pascal and Schopenhauer.

My retirement life now consists of writing, exercise, travel and meditation.

I am content.

출간된 도서 목록

삶의 보람을 찾아서 (ISBN# 9-781716-047152), lulu.com. 2022

삶의 보람을 찾는 여행 (ISBN 9-781387-546019).Lulu.com. 2023

난, 한국이 좋다 (ISBN 9-78131-268305). Lulu.com. 2023

Cruising Stories2 (ISBN 9-781312-541849) Lulu.com. 2023

그리운 대한민국 (ISBN# 9-781716-552502) lulu.com, 2021

물의 노래 (ISBN# 6-781716-605895). lulu.com, 2021

South America (ISBN # 9-781794-779587), lulu.com, 2021

Cruising Stories (ISBN# 9-781651-026748), lulu.com2020

From Korea to the World (ISBN# 978-1-537-42605-7), amazon.com, 2017

여행 이야기 5 (ISBN# 978-1-517-12352-9), amazon.com, 2016

오십 달러 미국유학 (ISBN# 978-1-522-85055-7), amzon.com, 2015

여행 이야기3 (ISBN# 978-1-503-18517-3), amazon.com, 2015

여행 이야기2 (ISBN# 978-1-496-05479-1), amazon.com, 2014

여행 이야기 (ISBN#978-1-489-59897-4). amazon.com, 2013

Traveling Stories (ISBN# 978-1-475-500156-3), amazon.com, 2013

Destiny of a Running Horse (ISBN# 978-1-453-76740-5), amazon.com, 2011

Dear Children (ISBN # 979-0-557-1458-4-3), amazon.com, 2009

새로운 청년을 위하여, 중앙 M&B, 2000

미국을 넘으면 한국이 보인다, 도서출판 이채, 1998

미국신문의 위기와 미래, 나남출판, 1998

하이! 닥터 장 , 벽호출판, 1997.

The Rise of Asian Advertising (with Teddy Palasthira and Hung Kyu Kim), Nanam: Seoul, Korea, 1995.

장박사와 미주리 언론마피아, Nanam: Seoul, Korea, 1995.

Mass Media in China: Its History and Future, Iowa State University Press: Ames, Iowa, 1989.

激變하는 新中國, 시사영어사, 1989. Mass Communication and Korea: A Global Perspective for Research, The Sungkok Foundation, Seoul, Korea, 1988.

www.ingramcontent.com/pod-product-compliance
Lightning Source LLC
Chambersburg PA
CBHW042209300626
47475CB00044B/539